Y0-AGK-015

ADVANCE PRAISE FOR
TOTAL INTERNSHIP MANAGEMENT

"An easily readable, step-by-step guide for any employer, backed by fresh and impressive data analyzing college student strengths and needs. This book will help employers build sustainable internship programs, and develop an effective college branding strategy."

— *Rusmir Music, Assistant Director of Experiential Programs, Brandeis University*

"Applying what they have learned in the classroom to real work experience is how students fast track their careers. Richard Bottner knows this first hand and has carefully crafted Total Internship Management as a "how to" for building successful internship programs. This book is a valuable and important tool for anyone who wants to help themselves, their organizations and the future workforce for many years to come."

— *Gael Keough, Director, University Relations, EMC Corporation*

"Solid internships will strengthen any college recruiting program, but it's hard work to do them right. Total Internship Management can help you get there."

— *Chris Resto, Co-author, RECRUIT OR DIE: How Any Business Can Beat the Big Guys in the War for Young Talent; Founding Director, UPOP, MIT's largest internship program*

"This book is the first that I have found that uses research to engage businesses in building the best internship programs possible."

— *James Westhoff Assistant Director and Internship Coordinator, Bowdoin College*

"A worthwhile read for companies considering an intern program."

— *David Almeda, Vice President, Human Resources, Staples, Inc.*

Total Internship Management

The Employer's Guide to
Building the Ultimate Internship Program

Richard Bottner

Second Printing

Intern Bridge, Inc.

Total Internship Management
The Employer's Guide to Building the Ultimate Internship Program

By Richard Bottner

© Copyright 2007 by Intern Bridge, Inc.
All Rights Reserved

ISBN 978-0-9799373-9-2

First Printing November 2007
Second Printing April 2008

All rights reserved. No part of this publication may be reproduced, stored in a retrieval system, transmitted, or shared by any means, electronic, mechanical, photocopying, recording, or otherwise, without the prior written permission of the publisher. For copyright permission, please email copyright@internbridge.com.

This publication is designed to provide accurate and authoritative information in regard to the subject matter covered. It is sold with the understanding that neither the author nor the publisher is engaged in rendering legal, accounting, or other professional service. If legal advice or other expert assistance is required, the services of a competent professional should be sought.

Further, although every precaution has been taken in the preparation of this book, the author and publisher assume no responsibility for errors or omissions. Nor is any liability assumed for damages resulting from the use of the information contained herein.

Published by Intern Bridge, Inc.
136R Main Street, Suite 3
Acton, MA 01720

For sales information, please email Sales@InternBridge.com or call us at 800-531-6091.

Cover design/layout/production: bookpackgraphics@yahoo.com (Dan Berger)

Printed in U.S.A.

ABOUT THE AUTHOR

Richard Bottner is the President and CEO of Intern Bridge, a college relations consulting, research and outsourced staffing organization. In 2006, Richard founded the New England Internship Study, the largest survey ever to be conducted solely on the topic of internships. Backed by this research, Richard has consulted for several organizations, helping them build effective internship programs based on student expectations. He has been invited to speak at numerous conferences including the National Association of Colleges and Employers, the Eastern Association of Colleges and Employers, the Mountain Pacific Association of Colleges and Employers, the New York State Cooperative and Experiential Education Association, and the New England Association for Cooperative Education and Field Experience.

Richard is also the founder of the Massachusetts Internship Council, a think-tank group aimed at building statewide internship strategies by bringing together universities, employers, and government agencies. He is the founder of the Total Internship Management national workshop series, and the weblog MillennialsGoToWork.com.

Richard is a member of the Northeast Human Resources Association where he serves on the College Relations Committee, the Eastern Association of Colleges and Employers where he is a member of the Business Interest Network, and the New England Association for Cooperative Education and Field Experience where he is a Massachusetts State Director.

He is also a member of the National Society for Experiential Education, the National Association of Colleges and Employers, the Society for Human Resources Management and the American Society for Training and Development.

Lastly, Richard is a proud member of the Millennial generation.

TABLE OF CONTENTS

INTRODUCTION

Staple that. Hang this. Collate these.

Unfortunately, these are my fondest memories of an internship I had while attending Babson College, a business school in Wellesley, Massachusetts, about 14 miles west of Boston. I had fell into the field of Human Resources after almost two years of trying to figure out what I ultimately wanted to do upon graduation. It was the fall semester of 2005 when I completed the college's Human Resources Management class, and realized it was something for which I had a growing passion.

At the time, I was enthusiastic and eager to learn more about the field. I approached my professor, a practicing leadership consultant with a great deal of experience and an enormous number of HR contacts. I explained that I was excited to have finally found a field that interested me, and I was looking for some "what now" guidance.

He quickly made two suggestions. The first was to join the regional HR association. He had given some presentations to their membership a few years prior, and felt that there was potential for me to assist with some of their professional development programs. His second suggestion was to obtain an HR internship for the spring semester. It sounded like great advice to me.

In the Career Development office, I explained to the director my newfound mission. Interestingly enough, she had spoken earlier that day with the people who managed the internship program in one of Boston's largest corporations, Byron Industries.[1] They mentioned that their popular business internships always had a high application rate, but they were trying to increase the applicant pool for their HR internship program. The Director handed me the flashy application which provided a detailed description of the company and the various HR internships that were being offered. I was impressed with the marketing materials and convinced that HR was my career goal. I feverishly completed the entire application later that night and sent it in the following morning. The semester was just concluding, and I was preparing to return to my home state of New Jersey for winter break.

As this was occurring, I was also making contact with the regional HR organization that my professor had discussed with me. They were intrigued by my interest and invited me for a meeting to discuss potential opportunities. I was to meet with the Executive Director and the Director of Conferences. As a junior in college, the chance to meet with executive level personnel from the

---

[1] Byron Industries and Delightful Desserts (mentioned later in the introduction) are fictitious names, representing the companies where I was an intern.

9

organization that represented my desired profession was, to say the least, very exciting.

I learned from the meeting that the organization hosted professional development seminars several times per month at various locations throughout the Metro Boston area. At least once per month, these programs were held at Babson. The headquarters for the HR association also happened to be located in the same town as the college. Normally, the Director of Conferences would have to travel back and forth from the office several times per day to manage the event. Realizing the inconvenience, the Executive Director and Conference Director were eager for me to help. The deal was that I would spend the entire day at the conference, including setup and breakdown, and in return I would have the chance to network with attendees, have lunch, and observe the actual programming. It was definitely a great arrangement. I was to begin my duties at the start of the spring semester in 2006.

I entered the winter recess with a great deal of hope that I had answered the college student's most feared question: "What will I do after the four years is up?" About a week into winter break I received a call from Byron. They left a friendly voicemail informing me that the organization was interested in interviewing me for a position in their spring 2006 internship program. The phone interview took place a few days later, and, not to my surprise, I was asked the sort of questions that my college's career development office had prepared me for.

With the expectation that I would work 12 to 15 hours per week at the downtown Boston office, I was offered an internship position in the Human Resources department. I would not earn a salary or wage, and it was required that I receive academic credit from Babson. I was told which sub-department of Human Resources I would be interning for, but not the specific work I would be doing. I was scheduled for an orientation session which was to take place the week before the official start of the spring internship program.

My experience at Byron left a lot to be desired; to say the least, my expectations were not met. At the start of the program, I was given a list of exciting tasks that I was to accomplish as part of my internship. However, I ended up spending most of my time hanging up flyers, collating, stapling, and filing. The amount of time that I actually spent performing non-menial tasks was at an extreme minimum. The internship was unpaid and I had to drive to and park in Boston. By the end of the internship, I had lost several hundred dollars on parking, gas, and tolls. Byron didn't even provide a parking stipend.

To make matters worse, Byron's overall culture was not supportive of an internship program. Interns were assigned to their respective departments, but every morning department leaders would send the internship coordinator an email if they needed an extra set of hands for the day. If an intern's supervisor gave permission, the intern would essentially be transferred for the day to an unfamiliar department, with no introduction, to complete – you guessed it – more menial tasks. I was transferred one day through this "intern marketplace" and my supervisor-for-a-day didn't even bother to ask my name. Instead, she referred to me as "intern." After conversing with my friends, who were interns within other organizations, it seemed that this was a widespread problem.

It was not until March of 2006, when I was two months into the Byron Industries internship that I realized there was an overall disconnect between employers and interns. On March 16th, 2006, I attended my third professional development seminar on behalf of the regional HR organization. The topic of the program was "Strategic Staffing." There were about fifty Human Resources personnel present, all of whom were at least at the manager level. The first half of the program focused on overall staffing strategies, and the second half of the program provided specific tools that organizations could use to implement the strategies. One of the main tools that the presenter suggested was an organization-wide internship program.

Since I was currently in an internship that I found less than satisfying, I was intrigued by his proposal and hoped that the HR professionals in the room could shed some light on my situation. To my surprise, the exact opposite occurred. The HR managers in the room looked dumbfounded, and proceeded to ask questions such as "Where do we find interns?" and "What kind of work should they do?"

Meanwhile, Byron Industries was investing a large amount of time and money into what they presumably thought was a successful program. Through hiring, training, and utilizing interns, the hope was that students would be ambassadors for their organization. But that was not going to happen with me. When friends asked what my internship was like, I told them how I truly felt. Friends that were thinking of applying to Byron Industries for an internship or full-time employment were told to reconsider. I was not trying to hurt the company; I was simply trying to be candid with my friends by telling them what I thought of the organization, a view that was based solely on my internship experience. I began to think that perhaps there was a large underlying problem when it came to organizations putting together internship programs for students.

I went home and immediately fired off an email to some of the Special Interest Groups of the HR association. That email started it all. I explained my situation and my observation during the professional development program. I threw out the idea of conducting research into internship management, hoping to receive just a few responses. The response was overwhelming. I received emails from several HR managers supporting the idea. As one HR manager wrote, "I would love to see a survey like this done and its results. I've been trying to figure out the 'formula' for college recruiting!"

Returning to my professor, I asked him if he would sponsor an independent research project for the following semester. He was excited about the idea and signed off on my research plan. Interestingly, the original plan was to research a small number of schools and organizations. I realized soon after starting the project that the plan was actually quite scalable. I thought "why not add more schools, if I can?" What was supposed to be a small survey ended up being one of the largest surveys to ever be conducted that focused solely on internships.

And then there was Delightful Desserts, my internship in summer of 2006. Delightful Desserts is in the foodservice business, operating hundreds of café-style establishments throughout the world. I worked in the training department; it was a truly excellent experience, mainly because I was given meaningful work assignments and had a terrific supervisor and great co-workers.

At the time I came on board, Delightful Desserts was rolling out a series of new products, and it was my job to update the training materials. "Updating" in most internships would probably mean taking the old page out of the training manual and replacing it with the one that someone else made. At Delightful Desserts, it was my responsibility to create brand-new training materials. To complete the task, I worked directly with high-level personnel from almost every department in the organization. By the end of the internship, I had overhauled almost all of the training materials and job aids that Delightful Desserts used in all of their stores.

My supervisor was great, as he took the time to understand what my abilities were. Ultimately, this saved him a great deal of time and made me as productive as I could be, thus allowing me to contribute significantly to the organization's bottom line. From day one, I was brought into the organization as an equal employee. My name was added to the "culture committee" list so when it came time in July to celebrate employee birthdays, my name was included on the giant card that sat next to the ice cream cake, and I received two movie tickets. My department also bought me a cake for a smaller party inside my supervisor's office. I was also given access to the employee discount on food I purchased. At the conclusion of the program, I even had lunch with the CEO. I left the organization with the utmost respect for how they view internships, student employment, and overall employee relations.

About six month later, I took a trip with friends to Florida. Delightful Desserts had just opened a new location in the airport. Missing their delicious food, I went over to place an order. As I watched the employees fill orders for the customers in front of me, I noticed that they were using the job aids and materials that I had created in Boston during the previous summer. It was extremely satisfying.

Here is the truly shocking part: Byron Industries hosted a highly-structured, substantial internship program that provided experiences to at least 40 students in each of the fall, spring, and summer semesters. The organization also employed two full-time individuals, with a large part of their responsibility dedicated to managing the program. On the other hand, Delightful Desserts did not have a formal program. They had occasionally hired interns, but it was not a steady flow or a highly structured program – yet they did it better and more effectively than an organization that was spending tens of thousands of dollars in salaries and opportunity costs.

The bottom line is that almost every organization can benefit from an internship program. As complicated as it might sound, once you've done it, it will become a seamless part of your organization's culture.

The information contained in this publication is largely based on the available data from the landmark Intern Bridge research. I hope that you will find the information in this publication interesting and useful. Furthermore, I hope you will leverage it within your organization. An internship program can be an incredible tool for creating a pipeline of fresh talent for your organization. Together, we can improve existing programs and create new ones that are positive and beneficial experiences for both the organization and the student.

Total Internship Management is a model I developed after countless hours of researching best practices, employers' perspectives, and the expectations and experiences of tens of thousands of students. It provides for a complete and thorough approach that all but guarantees students engaged within your organization for the purpose of workforce preparation will be provided with meaningful experiences. Ultimately, these experiences will lead to hugely positive, organization-wide results. I have seen it time and time again. The only thing that stands in the way of every organization managing experiential education correctly is the gap that exists between the organization, the university, and the student.

Let's bridge the gap.

METHODOLOGY OF OUR RESEARCH

Part of what makes this publication unique is that it is based on original, in-depth research into student and organizational experiences and expectations. The New England Internship Study collected responses from over 6,000 students from thirty universities, creating one of the largest internship research projects focused solely on the various areas of internship management. All of the statistics in this publication are from that landmark research.

The research data was collected using two surveys: one for students and one for organizations. The very first question on the survey for students was "Have you ever taken part in an internship experience?" Students who answered yes to this question were transferred to one set of questions, while students who answered no to this question were transferred to a different set of questions. Similarly, the very first question on the organizational survey was "Have you ever hosted an intern?" Individuals who answered yes to this question were transferred to one set of questions while others who answered no to this question were transferred to a different set. Using this method, each survey was actually two surveys in one. In essence, a total of four surveys were conducted. (Both surveys contained a certain number of questions that were answered by both groups without branching. These questions were mostly demographic in nature.)

The survey design was accomplished by reviewing existing surveys on similar topics. A group of local Human Resources representatives from various industries and companies of different sizes was also put together. This group conversed through email about several topics and questions they thought would be useful to be covered in the survey. The final questions were approved by this same group. The survey questions were then converted into an online format. All of the surveys were completed online using the Perseus survey software. Questions were both quantitative and qualitative in nature. The survey for organizations contained over 100 questions, while the survey for students contained between 50 and 100 questions (certain responses allowed the skipping of particular questions.)

With the cooperation of the Northeast Human Resources Association (NEHRA), the survey was distributed to HR professionals. NEHRA is the premiere association for Human Resources professionals in the New England area. The association has over 4,000 members representing companies throughout the business spectrum. The Executive Director emailed a memo containing a weblink to the survey to every member, asking for their participation. 246 organizations responded.

The aim of the project was to work with Human Resource professionals to improve internship programs. Once it was decided to survey organizations that were represented by NEHRA, it was agreed that the colleges given the opportunity to participate should be from the same region. It was further decided that four-year undergraduate colleges in Rhode Island, Massachusetts, and New Hampshire would be contacted. All colleges matching this criterion were invited to participate, regardless of affiliations, size, offered majors, or any other criteria. Universities were contacted through their Career Services Department. In all, 31 colleges representing 73,082 students participated, with 6,282 students responding.

An email, which included a link to the web survey, was created and sent to each college's Career Center, who then forwarded the email to their entire student body. (Please note that it was the decision of the individual student whether or not they wished to participate in the research, and it was not mandated by any school.) Because the original sample size was so large, it was impossible to have all the students take the survey on the same date. This would have overloaded the servers and crashed the survey system.

Therefore, the survey was distributed on a staggered basis during the fall 2006 semester. Two to three schools were sent the survey every other business day from October 15, 2006, through December 15, 2006. Prizes, donated by sponsoring organizations, were available to encourage student participation. The prizes, such as a $500 spring break gift certificate, a laptop, etc., were drawn randomly and awarded to student participants at the conclusion of the study.

IMPORTANT NOTE: There are over 100 student quotations in this publication, gathered directly from this research project. They are represented throughout this book by bold italicized quotations within shaded boxes. However, due to our obligations to student survey takers and universities, we are unable to publish the student's name, or which university they attend.

Participating Organizations

The following is a partial list of organizations who participated in this landmark research.

AAA Southern New England	Aigner Associates
AstraZeneca Pharmaceuticals	Alkermes
Blue Cross & Blue Shield of Rhode Island	Altus
	Atlantic Resource Group
Bose	Avecia Biotechnology Inc.
Boston Public Schools	BAO Inc.
Citizens Financial Group	Battenfeld Gloucester Engineering
Ecco USA, Inc.	Celerant Consulting
Federal Aviation Administration	Chestnut Hill Realty
Girl Scouts of Rhode Island	Coley Pharmaceutical Group
Hannaford Bros. Co.	Compensation Consulting Resources
John Hancock	Conquest Business Media
Lycos	Corporate Technologies
MA Medical Society	Eagle Tribune Publishing
Massachusetts Hospital Association	Earthwatch Institute
MetLife	ENSR
National Lumber	Equinox Group
New Balance Athletic Shoe, Inc.	Facing History and Ourselves
Ocean Spray Cranberries, Inc.	FM Global
Osram Sylvania, Inc, a Siemens Co.	Foster-Miller
Papa Ginos	Fuld & Company, Inc
PUMA North America, Inc.	Gazelle Strategic Partners, LLC
Staples	Gentle Giant Moving Company
Sun Life Financial	Getronics
Target Stores	Granite Telecommunications
Wyeth Biotech	Harpoon Brewery

Total Internship Management

Hartford Courant

HCPro

Hexagon Metrology, Inc

Hollingsworth & Vose Co.

Horn Group

Hudson Lock, LLC

Inanovate, Inc

Intellagents

Invensys Process Systems

JCSI

John Snow, Incorporated

KGA, INC.

Kirkland Albrecht & Fredrickson

Lexington Business Solutions

Lightbridge, Inc.

Looney & Grossman LLP

Madison Floral, Inc.

Marrakech, Inc.

May Institute, Inc.

Medical Information Technology, Inc. (MEDITECH)

Mettler-Toledo Process Analytics

MSPCA-Angell

NESI

New England Research Institute, Inc.

Noresco

NorthEast/Eagle Electric

Occupational and Environmental Health Network (OEHN)

OmniSonics Medical Technologies, Inc

Parkland Medical Center

Permabit

Phoenix Marketing International

Pine Street Inn

Pioneer

Pivot Solutions, Inc

Portland Press Herald Maine Sunday Telegram

PSG

Rainbow Worldwide Relocation & Logistics

Randstand

Redcats USA

Reynolds Resources

sdg Management Intelligence

SEPATON

Sepracor

Springwell

Staffing Solutions, Inc.

Stanley Bostitch

Strategic Resource Solutions, LLC

Taco, Inc.

TERI (The Educational Resource Institute)

The Village Bank

TNCI

UHY Advisors, NE, LLC

United Plastic Fabricating

ValleyWorks Career Center

Vega & Associates, Inc

Vermont Mutual Insurance Group

Vion Pharmaceuticals Group

Vitale Caturano & Company Ltd.

Wheelabrator Technologies Inc.

William Arthur

World Energy Solutions, Inc.

World Travel Holdings

Only organizations that provided advance permission have been listed.
The preceding is a list of participating organizations only,
and does not imply endorsement of this, or any other, Intern Bridge publication or service.

Participating Universities

The following is a list of universities who participated in this landmark research.

American International College

Assumption College

Babson College

Bentley College

Boston College

Brandeis University

Colby Sawyer

College of the Holy Cross

Curry College

Elms College

Emmanuel College

Framingham State College

Lasell College

Lesley College

Massachusetts Maritime Academy

Montserrat College of Art

Mount Ida College

Nichols College

Olin College

Pine Manor College

Regis College

Roger Williams University

Saint Anselm College

Southern New Hampshire University

University of New Hampshire

University of Rhode Island

Wentworth Institute of Technology

Westfield State College

Wheelock College

Worcester Polytechnic Institute

Worcester State College

Total Internship Management

THE MILLENNIAL GENERATION

Rachel I. Reiser
Principal, Understanding Millennials

The "Baby on Board" Generation

In December of 2006, two students in a transition-to-college course that I teach inquired about their final grades: they had each received an A- in my class. After I shared my grading methodology with the two of them, they were both thankful and appreciative of the information; one of them e-mailed me with apologies for bothering me with his inquiry, and explained that his generation had been conditioned to ask such questions and fight for the highest grade possible in all circumstances.

He wasn't wrong – his generation has been taught that as long as they try, their hard work and efforts will evidence themselves with only the highest of grades and other measures of success. In my role as a Class Dean who works with students to provide academic and personal support, I have a great deal of first-hand experience with the unique characteristics of this generation overall, and as a consultant on generation concerns, I have developed a pretty clear picture of how this psychography impacts their entree into the working world.

To most effectively recruit, retain, and motivate our newest employees, it is essential to understand not only who they are, but also the relevance of who they are. Remember the "Baby on Board" signs in cars in the '80s? Those babies on board grew up with a newfound attention to their needs, and they are today's college students and young employees – alternatively referred to as Echo-Boomers, Generation Y, Generation NeXt, and Millennial Generation – with ideas, issues, and ways of looking at the world different from 20-somethings a decade ago.

Who Are Millennials?

The first Millennials were born in 1982. In 2000 they graduated from high school, applied to colleges, enlisted in the military, and began voting. With the Millennial birth years ending in 2002, they are a large population – including immigration, they may end up being one-third larger than the Baby Boom Generation. They are also racially and ethnically more diverse than those that came before them.

Neil Howe and William Strauss (*Millennials Go to College*) believe that within a generation, people develop a "peer personality" in which they share events during their formative years, usually between 10 to 18 years old, that have an impact on their value system and psychographic profile as a group. At their essence, Millennials are highly achieving and highly programmed; they have been more nurtured and protected throughout their upbringing than any preceding generation.

They have been raised predominantly by Boomer Generation parents, although the youngest of them are being raised by early Generation Xers. Who their parents are is important, because they continue to play such a large role for Millennials through their college experience and into their professional lives. They have "helicopter parents," as termed by Wake Forest Dean Mary Gerardy because they are "always hovering." In an article published in the *Chronicle of Higher Education* (March 30, 2007) Strauss and Howe point out that "the core issue for graduate and professional schools will be job placement. Students and their Gen-X parents will expect institutions to provide opportunities for clinical work, apprenticeships, and career-related community service." The presence of the mom and dad loom large; they have engendered very specific qualities in their Millennial kids, and those qualities have substantial implications for how these young people will relate to the working world.

Seven Millennial Traits

Howe and Strauss detail seven core characteristics of Millennials, which may help us to understand them.

◆ Millennials are special.

And they've been told all their lives just how special they are. They had activities planned for them, their schedules were a family priority, and their every success was encouraged and praised. Consequently, they have extremely high expectations for themselves, and they hold others to the same standards. As they enter the job force, they will be increasingly demanding and place a higher expectation on internal customer service – the treating of employees the way that customers are treated. Additionally, they will care about their workplace and believe that they, as the new employees, are the ones who will bring in the fresh ideas and initiatives that will benefit all.

◆ Millennials are sheltered.

They have wonderfully close relationships with their families, and feel truly supported. They also struggle with disappointment, as they have in many cases been sheltered from such experiences throughout their formative years. With such protection, they haven't had much occasion to experience letdowns, and their coping skills are somewhat deficient as a result. They also have little experience figuring things out for themselves. Job recruitment professionals have been experiencing a sharp rise in the numbers of parents accompanying Millennial recruits on job interviews and contacting Human Resources for contract negotiations or to address on-the-job issues that their child may be experiencing.

◆ Millennials are confident.

As a 21-year old listener stated when calling into a discussion of "Generation Y at Work" on NPR's *On Point* on May 22, 2007, "I don't want to start from the bottom, and we've been told we don't have to." Because they came into the world at a time when children received new levels of attention and educational reform became a priority, they may be the smartest generation yet. Since being smart and successful is part of the Millennial personality, it has been elevated to "cool" status among this group, and they have every expectation that they will get the job title, perks, and pay that they want now, without "paying dues."

◆ Millennials are team-oriented.

Millennials have been working and doing in teams for as long as they can remember. In school, teams, activities, and jobs, Millennials have a long history of learning, working, and being evaluated in groups, which has worked well for them. As Claire Raines asserts in her 2002 web-article "Managing Millennials," "Millennials say they want to work with people they click with. They like being friends with coworkers. Employers who provide for the social aspects of work will find those efforts well rewarded by this newest cohort. Some companies are even interviewing and hiring groups of friends."

◆ Millennials are conventional.

They seek leadership, and even structure, from their older coworkers and managers, but they also expect that their ideas will be drawn out and respected. Millennial employees are used to loving parents who have made them the center of their lives and for whom they have great admiration and respect; they are looking for similar dynamics from their prospective employers. They want to look up to their manager, learn from him or her, and receive daily feedback. In working with Millennials, we need to be prepared to spend a lot of time teaching and coaching when hiring them.

◆ Millennials are pressured.

Young people worry more than ever about their future; we, in turn, worry about what this does to them. Studies show that many have never learned how to create balance in life, and as a consequence they have trouble sleeping and maintaining a reasonable schedule, staying healthy, and dealing with the normal hurdles of life. The confluences of their lack of coping skills and the dynamic of the relationship they share with their parents mean that we will continue to see the parents of young employees stepping in to address workplace stressors on behalf of their children. It is not unusual to hear of career educators or managers in corporate industry negotiating or working with the parents of their employees in addressing those employees' concerns.

◆ **Finally, Millennials are achieving**.
They see themselves as a generation of high achievers, and one negative result of this is that it can cause constant personal pressure and make them fearful of falling behind their peers. On the plus side, they have a deep understanding and working knowledge of technology, and they use this to their advantage. Great multitaskers, Millennials are busy at all times, and technology is a major tool for them as they try to keep up with it all. As discussed in the February 2006 article "Millennials Make Their Mark" published by Steelcase Inc., "More than any other generation, Millennials love technology. Theirs is the first generation raised with the internet, instant messaging and email. Other generations have adopted technology; Millennials were born into it." Unfortunately, this lifelong experience with technology may cause them to struggle with uncertainty and thus need immediate gratification. Moreover, prospective employers and managers have the challenge of understanding how Millennials approach using technology, and how it has formed them. As a young woman quoted in the Pew Internet & American Life Project (2001) puts it, "I get bored if it's not all going at once, because everything has gaps – waiting for an IM, waiting for a website to come up, commercials on TV, etc." This is quite a telling and concerning revelation regarding the attention span of the newest generation of employees.

So What?
The personality embodied by the Millennials calls for career educators and recruiters to rethink how we do what we do. We need to understand the Millennials' approach to the world, in particular what they expect of their professional opportunities and environments. To understand who these people are is an essential ingredient in working effectively with them. In our efforts to best cultivate and exploit the talents of prospective employees, we need to manage their expectations and help them to deal with stress and disappointment, all while capitalizing on their determination and talents. We also need to continue educating their parents about their own boundaries, and coach the would-be managers of these future employees on the unique dynamics that they bring to the table.

Howe and Strauss state "Millennials are already the most achievement-oriented collegians in our nation's history, and by the time they leave the campus gates, they may be the most learned and capable graduates ever." This is high praise and high pressure for a generation whose oldest representatives are in their early 20s.

In a career spanning over 15 years in higher education, Rachel has held positions at several schools where she worked directly with college students, providing her with the opportunity to experience first hand the changing characteristics of today's late adolescent, and fostering her professional interest in generational studies. She is currently the Associate Dean of Academic Services at Babson College. Rachel has researched, written, and presented extensively on the demographics and psychographics of the generation born between 1982 and 2002. She has presented countless programs on this topic to a range of audiences and has served as a consultant to groups and organizations in helping them to consider their work in the age of the Millennial Generation. She can be contacted at rreiser@babson.edu

HOW MILLENNIALS DIFFER FROM BOOMERS AND GENERATION X

Boomers (1943-1960)	Gex X (1961-1981)	Millennials (1982-2002)
Fought for the systematic dismantlement of adult protectiveness	Grew up feeling neglected and overlooked, latchkey kids	Grew up feeling important and cared for, often overprotected
Raised by parents with Dr. Spock-style nurturing tolerance	Raised with great personal freedom	Raised in groups under adult supervision
Idealistic	Cynical and alienated	Optimistic
At the helm of an intense and influential cultural youth rebellion	Question authority	Follow Rules
Want meaningful lives, careers, experiences, etc.	Self-absorbed	Team-oriented
Thought to be midway through a multifaceted reworking of society	Slackers	Held in high regard with high expectations of their future contributions to society

Some Suggested Readings:

- Brooks, D. "The Organization Kid." *The Atlantic Monthly,* April 2001.
- Carlson, S. "The Net Generation Goes to College." *The Chronicle of Higher Education,* October 2005.
- Howe, N. & Strauss, W. Millennials Rising: *The Next Great Generation.* New York: Vintage Books, 2000.
- Howe, N. & Strauss, W. *Millennials Go To College.* LifeCourse Associates, 2003.
- Kantrowitz, B. & Typr, P. "The Fine Art of Letting Go." *Newsweek,* May 22, 2006.
- Kindlon, D. *Too Much of a Good Thing: Raising Children of Character in an Indulgent Age.* New York: Hyperion Books, 2001.
- Lancaster, L. & Stillman, D. *When Generations Collide.* New York: HarperColllins Publishers, Inc., 2002.
- Langfitt, F. "Startups Help Clean Up Online Reputations." *NPR Online.* URL: http://www.npr.org/templates/story/story.php?stroyId=6462504, November 16, 2006
- Mosier, A. "Millennials Floating." *First Things.* December 2001, 118.
- O'Briant, D. "Millennials: The Next Generation." *The Atlanta Journal-Constitution,* August 2003.
- Raines, C. "Managing Millennials." *Generations at Work.* URL: http://www.generationsatwork.com/articles/millenials.htm, 2002.
- Sacks, D. "Scenes from the Culture Clash." *Fast Company.,* January 2006, 102.

In an effort to provide you with the opportunity to implement an internship program as an internal process, the most important steps are outlined below and continued on Page 28. Please note that this should serve only as a "quick reference" and the chapters should be read in-depth to gain a true understanding of Total Internship Management.

QUICK REFERENCE GUIDE TO TOTAL INTERNSHIP MANAGEMENT

STEP 1: Does you organization have what it takes?

Conduct an organizational audit. **(Page 45)**

Gain executive level support. **(Page 46)**

Achieve an understanding of why your organization desires to host interns. **(Page 31)**

Learn why students may pursue an internship with your organization. **(Page 37)**

STEP 2: Create the program structure

Determine the best semester(s) for your organization and students. **(Page 49)**

Create an intern work plan that expresses the work a student will complete. **(Page 53)**

STEP 3: Select which departments and individuals will act as supervisors

Decide which department(s) will receive interns. **(Page 61)**

Determine, based on the ideal traits that an intern supervisor in your organization should possess, who will supervise each intern. **(Page 61)**

STEP 4:
Build a compensation and benefits plan for interns (Page 95)

STEP 5: Market your internship program to students

Choose the most appropriate universities to target the program. (Page 67)

Establish partnerships with the targeted colleges. (Page 69)

Implement a marketing plan based on pre-determined strategies. (Page 72)

STEP 6: Interview and selection

Build a list of appropriate behavioral interview questions. (Page 78)

Screen and select candidates based on a pre-determined rubric of desired intern qualities. (Page 81)

STEP 7: Orientation programming

Work with students to help them become acclimated to your organization. (Page 85)

Communicate to employees the positive influence an internship program can have, and their role in the process. (Page 86)

STEP 8: Evaluations

Conduct evaluations of student's performance and provide feedback. (Page 105)

Provide students with the opportunity to provide feedback. (Page 93)

DEFINING YOUR
INTERNSHIP PROGRAM

On the surface this probably appears to be a simple task. But if you ask different groups their opinion on how to define an internship program, you are guaranteed to receive highly conflicting responses. Students' perception of an internship will differ from organizations', and vice versa. The disparity increases when taking into consideration the different sizes of organizations and the industries they do business in, as well as the varying sizes of colleges and the degree programs they offer.

The idea of "brain drain" gains significant meaning when examined through the lens of workforce development and experiential education. Brain drain is the general concept of knowledgeable, well-educated individuals migrating from a specific geographic area and taking their talent elsewhere. Every year, hundreds of thousands of college seniors graduate and move back to their home states, or another region where they were offered employment. When this occurs, the region where the university is located loses out on the economic benefits that would have been realized had the student stayed. This is a brain drain. Across the nation, more and more regions are recognizing that they have a serious problem retaining young, energetic talent. Not surprisingly, regionally-sponsored internship programs have consistently been one of the most broadly used, and most successful, initiatives taken to combat the brain drain problem.

Intern Bridge was recently invited to attend a brain drain prevention meeting sponsored by a local state government. At this meeting, a collection of individuals representing businesses, universities, and the state government gathered to discuss how to implement some sort of a plan that would generate internships in the region. The hope was that if more students took part in an internship program, they would network and seek employment in the state upon graduation. What we learned as the meeting progressed was that this process had been occurring for the past four years with little result. After digging deeper into the problem, the reason why the group was finding it so difficult to put a strategy into action became apparent: the colleges and businesses could not come to an agreement on the definition for an internship.

Granted, there really is no true "one size fits all" definition for an internship. There are, however, some statements and generalizations that we can say about these experiences which at least allow us to have a shared understanding of their purpose and place in both business and career development.

Internships Are...

Internships are structured, supervised, and short-term programs in which undergraduate or graduate students perform tasks and duties within an organization in order to gain knowledge and experience. The internship is usually performed over the course of one semester, or during a summer or winter break. The student may or may not earn monetary compensation from the company and/or academic credit from their university. Internship programs should benefit both the student and the organization.

Internships Are Not...

Internships are typically not repeated by the same student. They are also not an opportunity to hire part-time or full-time free labor to perform tasks that other employees do not have time or desire to complete. Internships must have an educational component. In our survey, one HR representative wrote that an intern is a "sub-entry-level temporary position," while another professional wrote that an internship is "when a student performs duties related to their studies for little or no compensation." Neither of these statements present the right approach to an internship program.

Internships vs. Co-ops

Intern Bridge frequently receives requests for clarification on the distinction between internships and co-ops. Cooperative education, also known as a Co-op, is very similar to internships. However, co-ops usually link more closely to the academic institution. They are typically intensive full-time positions, and almost always part of a program that will allow the student to receive academic credit from their university by participating in seminars and completing essays. While an intern may work full-time during the summer months, most interns who work during the academic year do so on a part-time basis. Co-ops are often part of a five-year degree program and can last an entire year, instead of just one semester. While this research is predominately focused on internships, much of the information can be applied to co-ops as well.

Is an Organized Internship Program Really That Important?

Yes! When an intern leaves your organization they will either become an ambassador or adversary. This outcome is largely dependant on how well your organization executes the processes outlined in this guide. The job and internship search are the primary activities of college students, and therefore a chief topic of conversation among friends and families. Students *will* talk about their experiences; whether or not they have good things to say comes down to the dedication of your organization. Giving interns a great experience in an organization has huge long-term benefits, such as great public relations on the intern's campus, as well as an edge when it comes time to recruit for full-time positions.

While well-organized and effective internship programs have the potential to greatly benefit a company, it is important to remember that unorganized programs have their consequences as well. 92% of surveyed professionals agreed that an internship could help the recruiting brand of an organization; yet only 29% thought that an internship program has the potential to hurt the recruiting brand. Of the students who reported having taken part in an internship, 96% agreed that they had shared their experiences with friends, and 99% of students who had not yet taken part in an internship agreed that they would share experiences with friends. This is one of the largest disconnects between organizations and students, which should caution organizations that a lack of knowledge and preparation could yield negative returns in recruiting talent.

PURPOSE FOR ORGANIZATIONS

This section seeks to provide information for the many reasons that organizations should consider hosting an internship program.

> *"I BELIEVE an internship is an unbelievable experience. It helps you get your foot in the door. I had completed an internship through my high school and loved it so much, it turned into my job! And I've been working there for 3 years this month!"*

Identify Future Hires

One of the most common reasons HR professionals say they host internship program for is the opportunity to identify potential full-time employees. Depending on the structure and size of your organization, an internship may fit in perfectly with your succession planning. As employees are promoted through the organization, interns (many of whom are soon-to-be seniors who will be seeking employment) could be perfect candidates to fill entry-level positions.

Conduct Recruiting Activities with Low Risk

There are few other scenarios where an individual participates in a twelve week long "interview" and where the organization can simply say "goodbye" at the end with no strings attached. Internships provide the opportunity for organizations to do just this. So long as you provide interns with the opportunity to learn, chances are that they will be satisfied with their overall experience. In that case, everyone goes home a winner: the student is able to gain workplace education and the organization is able to avoid a hiring blunder.

Provide Supervisory Experience

Internship programs can provide supervisory experience for an employee who has little experience in this area. It allows the employee to practice these skills on just one person. As we will learn later, interns should be evaluated consistently. Using this method, it is easy to learn about potential problems with the supervisor and to coach that person through the learning process.

Pipeline for Additional Candidates

Even if an intern declines an offer for a repeat internship or full-time employment, that student can provide a pipeline for additional candidates. Students who pursue internships are often connected to their campus community in some manner: through a professor, the career office, an administrator, or maybe a student club. By working to create long-lasting relationships with interns, an organization can almost guarantee to have a steady flow of applications.

Gain Short Term Talent

Your organization may have a special project coming up that requires a skilled individual with a special area of expertise. While some individuals may look to the aid of a consultant, doing so is often prohibitively expensive. Interns can often provide a great deal of valuable talent for these special projects.

Provide The Organization with Fresh Ideas

Everyone seems to want a piece of the training budget pie. Imagine the opportunity to bring someone to the table who has had a long, steady period of job-specific training. Interns have been applying themselves in academic programs for several years. They possess an incredible amount of up-to-date knowledge, and are a valuable source of fresh ideas. You must remember that interns are often able to articulate new industry ideas and concepts learned in the classroom in a manner that individuals who have been out of school for many years may struggle with. In particular, today's students are unafraid of technology and can be great assets in technology-related projects.

Increased Retention Rate

Students who are hired to work full-time in an organization where they were once interns are more likely to stay with the organization for a longer period of time. These employees are familiar with the culture, structure, and work of the organization. They also require little orientation or training once hired for the full time position.

Provide Students with Real Work Experience

Students seek real work experience when taking part in an internship program. Organizations effectively provide students with a chance to gain this experience. The structure of the program ultimately determines if students gain "real work experience," but once this is achieved, the results are high-impact for the student's development, the organization's mission and goals, and the local economy and workforce development.

Reinvigorate the Work Force

Interns are youthful, usually much more so than the majority of the employees in the organization. Their presence alone often has a refreshing affect on the workforce, and overall productivity may even increase.

Low-Cost Labor and No-Cost Labor

This is the purpose that students hate to hear and organizations don't really like to admit. Yes, one reason for hosting an intern is to provide your organization with a source of well-educated labor on the cheap. It may even be okay to have this expectation. Organizations, generally speaking, acquire interns at a much lower cost of labor than temporary, part-time, or full-time employees. From recruiting to compensation to benefits, it simply costs less.

The major problem is when this purpose becomes the main purpose, or even worse, the only purpose. Hiring an intern just because it is a chance to put the breaks on labor costs is by far a worse practice. Further, if your organization approaches internship programs with this mentality it will damage relationships with universities and, ultimately, they will cease to send interns to your organization's program.

Completing Work that Employees Don't Have Time or Desire To Do

Personnel can always use an extra set of hands. It is understandable that there is necessary work that full-time employees simply do not have time to complete. Some organizations choose to hire temporary employees to solve this problem; others have deep enough pockets to pay significant overtime or extra salaries. The real problem occurs when the purpose of hosting an internship program becomes to complete work that full-time employees do not want to do. As with labor costs, this cannot become the primary goal of an internship program.

> *"SOMETIMES I felt like I wasn't as respected as the rest of the employees and that people just threw projects at me that they had no interest in doing, instead of choosing ones that would be best for my learning experience."*

To Be a "Good Human Resources Organization"

Internships are gaining popularity by leaps and bounds. As the economy continues to improve, organizations are able to apply more time and resources towards their recruiting function, including internships.

Build Relationships with Local Colleges

For many reasons, building relationships with local colleges can be extremely important to your organization. Most importantly, it provides you with the chance to network directly with the individuals who can give you access to a wide range of talented young people. By building relationships with colleges, you are also opening the door for the institution to become involved with your organization, acting as consultants, guest speakers, and more. Hosting an internship program gives your organization the "in" and provides invaluable advertising.

Hosting an Internship Is Good For Public Relations

Providing for an internship program may lend itself to generating media for your organization. In the literature review portion of the research, hundreds of newspaper and magazine articles focusing on the structure of the program, spotlighting a particular intern, or announcing some sort of major organization-wide development accomplished by an intern were obtained. Internships, when hosted correctly, have the power to boost an organization's reputation through the power of the press.

Increase Diversity

It is important to understand that diversity internship programs are growing quickly in numbers. Organizations such as InRoads are coupling experiential education with diversity. Students travel from all parts of the country and the world. For example, Babson brings students together from 26 states and 35 countries. Tapping into local colleges for interns is a tremendous opportunity to add diversity to the workforce. For more information about diversity internships, see the chapter in this publication.

Assistance with Projects to Free-Up Full-Time Employees

Project overload is an unfortunate occurrence in organizations. With the help of interns, smaller projects can be completed while more experienced full-time personnel can move on to projects that require a greater deal of specialized skill.

Work Opportunities for Employees' Children

While an internship program should not be implemented to serve as a "baby-sitting" service, it is worthwhile to note that there can be additional sources of intern candidates other than just your local universities. The caveat to this is that children of employees rarely stay with the organization long-term, which is one of the main reported reasons to host an internship program. Depending on the culture of your organization, the internal politics relating to hiring employees' children can also become problematic.

SURVEY DISCUSSION

Table A shows the ranked survey data for reasons why organizations choose to host internship programs. Column A represents organizations that have not yet hosted an internship program. Column B represents organizations that have hosted an internship program. This format allows for a comparison between the two groups.

A	Table A	B
1	Identify future hires	2
2	Provides students with real work experience	1
3	To be a good human resources organization	10
4	Build relationships with local colleges	3
5	Conduct recruiting activities with low risk	9
6	Gain short term talent	4
7	Hosting an internship program is good for public relations	7
8	Work needs to be completed that current employees do not have time to do	5
9	Provide the organization with fresh ideas	6
10	Increase diversity within my organization	8
11	Low-cost labor	12
12	No-cost labor	14
13	Reinvigorate the current work force	11
14	Completing work that employees don't have time or desire to do	13
15	Other organizations host interns, so my organization feels obligated to host interns too	15

PROBLEMATIC RESPONSES

Other organizations host interns, so the organization feels obligated to host interns too.

There were 12 respondents who answered "a great extent" or "a very great extent" to this topic. Organizations should not host interns solely on the basis of a perceived obligation.

Low-cost labor and no-cost labor.

Looking closer at the data, 38 survey takers in total from both groups had agreed to a "great extent" or "a very great extent" that No Cost Labor was a purpose for hosting an intern. More than 60% of these responses came from organizations who have not hosted interns. While 38 individuals may not sound like a lot, it represents 38 different organizations who may host more than one intern, and who may be setting themselves up for disappointment. Again, low-cost labor and no-cost labor can be purposes for hosting interns – but absolutely not on their own.

Completing work that employees don't have time or desire to do.

A total of 23 survey takers from both groups had agreed to a "great extent" or "a very great extent" that employees lacking desire to complete certain work was a motivating factor for hosting interns – a scary fact. The kinds of activities that employees do not want to participate in are usually the mundane ones such as stapling, collating, and filing; it would be a major disservice to the organization to farm these activities out as sole objectives in an internship program.

PURPOSE FOR STUDENTS

This section seeks to provide information for the many reasons that students pursue participation in an internship program. By gaining the perspective of a student, your organization can plan and implement an internship program capable of truly delivering experiences that exceed student expectations.

> *"IN ORDER for an internship to be meaningful I think the intern needs to walk away from it having enjoyed the time they spent, having gained knowledge and experience, maybe some contacts, and, in a perfect world, a job. That's what internships are for, right?"*

Gain Real Work Experience

While a college education docs provide valuable theory, it does not always prepare students for the transition of applying theory learned in the classroom to real-world scenarios. This skill can only be gained by experiencing the work environment. Students engaged in an internship program have the opportunity to build upon classroom theories to make real decisions and solve relevant problems.

> *"THEY PROVIDED real work experience in an environment where learning was encouraged and contacts could be made."*
>
> *"SOMETIMES I felt like I wasn't as respected as the rest of the employees and that people just threw projects at me that they had no interest in doing, instead of choosing ones that would be best for my learning experience. "*
>
> *"I WAS able to apply my college textbook learning to actual cases."*
>
> *"I REALLY enjoyed the ability to get a sense for how theoretical knowledge I gain in school is applied to practical work in everyday situations."*
>
> *"AS LONG as I'm learning and gaining knowledge and experience, then I find the experience meaningful."*

Learn New Skills

Many students enjoy the chance to learn a new set of skills. While they may enter an internship with a particular skill set, there is the expectation that students will have the chance to either learn brand new skills or build upon an existing skill.

> *"I FEEL as though internships are an excellent way for students to gain experience and knowledge in their specific area of study. I believe that hands-on training is the absolute best and most efficient way for a student to learn. There are a lot of careers in the real world. I would love to see what is out there, and I would especially like to examine which career I would excel at. I have a lot of great ideas, and would love to share them!"*
>
> *"WHAT I liked most about my internship was the freedom and chance to work with minimal supervision. Also the knowledge gained was incredible – more so than what I could have learned in any college classroom."*

Build the Resume

College students can expand upon their resume in only a handful of ways. One of the primary methods of "fattening up" the resume is to participate in an internship. There is also an unquantifiable degree of expectation by family, universities, and future employers that a student should participate in at least one internship. Some students will complete two, three, or even more internships.

"THE PROFESSIONAL environment of the organization was really great and the fact that I could use my experience and contacts as resume builders afterwards was important."

"I LIKED the items that I was able to add to my resume and talk about in interviews. I also liked that it gave me an idea of what people do in different jobs to help me decide what profession I want to go into."

Make New Connections/Network

Making connections serves as another primary reason why students seek internship experiences. Students often hear about the power of networking throughout their university education, but do not get a chance to practice it as a skill. An internship provides students with this opportunity through the social setting of a professional organization. Students will therefore understand the importance of expanding their network beyond family members and friends.

"I WAS able to establish many contacts with prominent people in the finance industry."

"WHAT I liked most about my internship was the countless opportunities to network, and [the] relationships with other interns."

Experience Work With a Potential Full-Time Employer

One reason that organizations host internships is to screen potential hires. Students are no different. They will take part in an internship at an organization where they may be interested in obtaining full-time employment. They are essentially screening the organization for the kind of work and environment that they will be subject to if they were to accept a full-time position of employment.

"I THINK an internship would be great and I pray that I have a wonderful experience with mine when the time comes. I look forward to getting the inside scoop on the place I want/hope to work at before being committed. It will also help many people to get a foot in the door at their dream work place."

"I GOT to do a variety of things, and they weren't menial jobs. I was actually a critical member of the team."

Receive a Full-Time Job Offer from Employer

While not usually a chief motivating factor, students do participate in internship programs with the hopes of receiving a full-time job offer when they are finished. If a student receives positive evaluations throughout the program, the expectation is, depending on the organization, that a job offer will follow.

Complete Interesting and Challenging Tasks

Some students enjoy being spoon-fed concepts and ideas, while other students love to be challenged. Give them an assignment and they will keep working on it until the job is done. An internship gives the self-motivated student a chance to be stimulated through interesting and challenging tasks.

> *"I LIKED learning about different types of work and what is involved. Learning about what my co-workers/supervisors did on a daily basis really allowed me to think about whether I could do that job everyday."*

Earn Money

All students want it, and some students need to have it. The discussion of whether you supply interns with monetary compensation will come up later in this publication, but you should know that the demand certainly exists. Expectations have grown that internships are a chance to earn money. Rumors have spread on campuses that some interns receive hourly pay of over $30. Of course, every student now wants to be paid at that rate.

Many students whole heartedly believe that they deserve to be compensated monetarily for their work, and many of these students will not accept an internship unless it is paid. Other students simply need to earn money for life expenses such as rent, tuition, books, car payments, etc. Some students do receive scholarships as well as federal grants and loan money. However, for many students this is simply not enough. These students seek paying internships because they need to be paid in order to complete their degree. It is always considered a best practice to offer interns monetary compensation.

Test Out a New Organization or Industry

Students are rarely exposed to the working side of various industries before they attend college. The four years they spend in college provide them with an opportunity to explore new industries and career paths. Internships are often used to gain insight into a particular organization or industry. For example, being a business student is versatile: business students can take their degrees to a multitude of different industries, but picking which industry to work in is not easy.

"THE LOCATION and type of work I was doing was different. I spent the summer in a different part of the country doing a completely new type of work."

"I LEARNED a lot about the industry—but most of all I learned that it was not what I want to do for a career. I liked it and had a great time, but I wasn't passionate enough about it."

By the time some students graduate, they will have experienced work in five, six, or as many as ten different industries. Some students have a more drastic shift as a result of participating in an internship. A story comes to mind from one student who was committed to the criminal justice program at a local university for over two years before an internship in the sales department of an electronics retailer changed his academic major and career path.

Fulfill Degree Requirements

This is a growing trend in United States universities. Several degree programs are now requiring that students take part in an internship. This used to be the case only with specific programs such as nursing, psychology, engineering, and education. More and more schools, however, are mandating that students complete internships for business, computer science, communication, and graphic design degrees – just to name a few. As this trend continues to grow, the pool of students looking for an internship will also grow. By implementing an internship program now, or by improving your existing program, your organization will be better prepared as colleges increase emphasis on experiential education.

Receive College Credit

Receiving college credit is different from an internship that is necessary to fulfill degree requirements. In the former case, the student is electing to pursue an internship in order to receive academic credit that they would not receive otherwise. Students typically do this for two reasons: first so that they can take a reduced course load during the school year. If they receive four credits for their internship experience, those are four less credits they need to achieve in the classroom.

The second reason is to broaden their transcript. If they are receiving academic credit for the internship, it will appear on their transcript as "experiential education," "internship seminar," or another variation. Universities that grant academic credit for internships tend to pay more attention to the actual content of the internship itself than schools that do not. When the student is not receiving credit, the university may have less involvement.

Take Part in Community Service

For civic-minded students, there are few activities more worthwhile than giving back to the community. Many students specifically seek internships in the not-for-profit sector hoping for a chance to make a difference either in their own community, somewhere else domestically, or even internationally. For example, one Boston university offers the opportunity for business students to travel to disadvantaged countries around the world to teach business competencies for the summer. Many not-for-profit organizations, both small and large, offer some type of internship program.

> *"IT WAS rewarding to help children with special needs."*
>
> *"THE PEOPLE I worked with were dedicated and sincere. I felt like I was making a positive, important impact on peoples' lives and I could see that positive change directly manifested in the work I performed."*
>
> *"AT THE end of the day I felt really good about what I had done, and how many kids I had helped. I liked watching my students' progress over the course of the sessions. I liked the interaction I had with the students and the other employees."*

Have a Fun and Entertaining Semester or Summer

Some students are in it just for the fun. After a long day or week of grueling classes, some students just want the chance to unwind and do something entertaining. While few students turn to internships to fill this void, it further drives home the point that internships cannot simply be clerical or mundane in nature.

> *"I LIKED the people that I worked with. All of them were extremely welcoming to a college kid with very little work experience. They treated me as part of the team, which I really liked, and they were fun to be around for 7 hours a day."*

Live in a Specific Area

While living in a specific area is not usually the main reason why a student seeks an internship, it is certainly a consideration. Some students have never left their hometown region and are interested in what other parts of the country have to offer. This may not compel you to market your internship to schools several hundred miles away (unless you have a large internship program, of course), but don't be surprised if you receive applications from students whose home addresses are several states away.

"MY INTERNSHIP was in Ireland!"

"I GOT the chance to live in Boston."

"MY INTERNSHIP was a wonderful experience because it was located in San Francisco."

"I REALLY enjoyed living in the Washington, D.C. area and learning a lot about the life that is lived down there by so many in our country. I enjoyed working side-by-side with so many people in the political arena."

SURVEY DISCUSSION

Table B (on Page 44) shows the ranked survey data for reasons why students pursue internship programs. Column A represents students who have not yet taken part in an internship program. Column B represents students who have taken part in an internship program. This format allows for a comparison between the two groups.

A	Table B	B
1	Gain real work experience	1
2	Learn new skills	3
3	Build resume	2
4	Make new connections/network	5
5	Experience work at a potential full-time employer	6
6	Receive a full-time job offer from employer	10
7	Complete interesting and challenging tasks	4
8	Earn money	9
9	Test out a new organization or industry	7
10	Receive college credit	11
11	Have a fun and entertaining semester or summer	8
12	Required to fulfill degree requirements	13
13	Take part in community service	14
14	Live in a specific area	12

Money Does Not Come Out On Top

One of the most interesting pieces of data to come out of this portion of the research is where "earning money" fell in the ranking. Positions 8 and 9 shed a great deal of light on one of the largest apprehensions that organizations have about hosting interns. From this data we can learn that so long as many of the items ranked higher than earning money are fulfilled, students may be willing to accept less monetary compensation. The vast majority of reasons ranked higher than earning money are content- and structure-based, proving that you can have a successful and beneficial internship program without being tremendously concerned with monetary compensation, provided you work to ensure that your program is academically sound.

Does Your Organization Have What It Takes?

The truth is not every organization is fit to be an effective host for an internship program. There are several factors that you need to consider to make sure that your organization is suitable. Consider a brief "organizational audit." As opposed to other business audits, one that focuses on an organization's ability to host an internship program will only take a few minutes and should include an analysis of some key internship-related issues.

Organizational Audit

The Organizational Audit was originally printed in The Internship as Partnership by Bob Inkster and Roseanna Ross (published by the National Society for Experiential Education in 1998.) In consultation with the authors, we offer the following revised list.

How serious is my organization about hosting an internship program?
- Is my organization committed to working with universities?
- Will my organizational culture be supportive of an internship program?

What can interns do for us? What are our goals?
- Does my organization have meaningful work for interns to complete?
- Are there special technical skills we need in interns?
- Do we want to use the internship program to identify, test, and recruit interns as potential new employees?
- Would an intern's naiveté and inexperience actually be an asset for our organization, providing a fresh perspective on our products or services? Or would a naïve intern actually be dangerous to self and to others in certain positions?

What human resources do we have to support an intern?
- Can my organization provide an individual with efficient supervisory skills to work with interns?
- Can my organization provide an individual with sufficient time to organize the program?
- In which departments might interns work?

Does my organization have the time to support an intern?
- What is the best time of year for my organization to host interns?
- What should the duration of individual internships be?

What physical resources do we have to support an intern? For example,
- A safe, adequate workspace
- Access to computers
- Internet access
- Telephone and fax
- Other communication resources
- Adequate reference resources • Parking
- Access to people who would be colleagues, resources, or internal clients

What financial resources do we have?

- Will my organization be able to afford to pay a salary to interns? If so, how much?
- What remuneration, instead of salary, can we provide? (Parking, stipend, etc.)

EXECUTIVE INVOLVEMENT

Executives are the leadership and role models of an organization. It is extremely important to gain their support for an internship program. All successful internship programs in major organizations stem from executive buy-in; and executive buy-in with regard to an internship program must be more than just approving the funds to build the program's financial foundation.

Here are some ideas to show how executives can support an internship program:

- Have an organization-wide communication piece sent directly by an executive to all of the employees within the organization announcing the launch or improvement plan of the internship program. A simple email is highly effective. Don't miss out on this easy opportunity to provide executive support to a program.
- Have executives welcome interns on their first day.
- Provide an opportunity for interns to have lunch with an executive.

"THE PLACE where I interned was not a good place for interns to work. It was a small company and they didn't take the time to show me around. They just pushed the interns aside."

"THE CULTURE was positive for interns – respect, professional behavior, and meaningful work were all a part of my experience."

"THE CULTURE of the firm was unbelievable."

"I LOVED the environment and the amount of responsibility put on me. I felt as though I played a role in the company and wasn't just an intern."

"I LIKED the overall environment of the office the best. All of my co-workers were supportive, hard-working, and became great friends of mine."

Remember, it is highly unlikely that your program can be a success without this vital component. Once you gain executive involvement, make sure to keep them in the loop about developments within your program, especially with examples of how interns are providing value to the organization.

STRUCTURING AN INTERNSHIP PROGRAM

The manner in which you choose to structure your internship program is extremely important. Structure is, by far, one of the key ingredients to a successful internship program.

Choosing A Semester

There are four general time frames when students attempt to obtain an internship. These times are typically in line with the academic calendar and are broken down into two categories: when classes are in session, and when classes are not in session.

Summer and Winter Semesters

The summer semester starts when students complete their final exams. Each school has its own academic calendar, but in most institutions this process is complete by the second week of May. The summer concludes when classes begin again in the fall, usually meaning the last week in August or first week of September. Students typically request at least one week on each end of the internship to take a vacation or prepare for upcoming activities. Therefore, most students have between twelve and fourteen weeks in the summer to work at an internship site. With the summer being the most popular time students seek internships, the candidate pool will also be the largest for this period. Summer internships have the potential to allow the student to work with the organization for the longest length of time, allowing the organization to accomplish larger, more long-term projects.

The winter semester is the time between the completion of final exams from the fall semester and the start of classes in the spring semester. Hosting an internship program during the winter semester tends to be tricky. The time period is extremely brief (three to six weeks), depending on the university. You will be competing with family vacations and the holiday season. Some students just want a break during the winter session. The pool of potential candidates for winter semester internships will be at its lowest. However, winter semester internships do lend themselves nicely to short-term special projects. It may be best to reserve winter session internships for students who have already been interns within your organization since they have already become acclimated to the environment. In addition, many schools will not recognize such a brief internship for academic credit.

Students ranked a summer internship as the most desired. Organizations, based on work available for interns, also ranked summer as the best time to host interns.

Fall and Spring Semesters

From a student's perspective, there is not a large difference between taking part in an internship program in the fall or spring semesters. Students will be enrolled and participating in their academic institutions during these time periods. Interns will be attending classes where instructors will assign them homework and often obligate them to take part in group work. Furthermore, students may be playing a part in school clubs, activities, and perhaps working another job to financially support themselves. As a result of these other commitments, it can be slightly more difficult to host interns during the fall and spring semesters.

On the other hand, some students will take part in an internship in lieu of a class during the school months. While this type of activity is traditionally more of a co-op (not directly covered in this publication), some students will connect a part-time internship experience to an independent study project or a university-administered internship seminar course to earn academic credits.

How Much Time Can I Expect Interns to Commit to My Organization?

The amount of time that an intern has to work for your organization is largely dependant upon which semester you choose to host the program. As previously stated, students will have less time to work when classes are in session. As shown by the data, the majority of past interns would prefer to work between 1 and 20 hours per week during the semester. Students who are taking classes will not have time to perform high quality work for your organization much more than 20 hours per week.

Based on the data for summer and winter, it can be observed that when classes are not in session, students are willing to work more hours. A closer look at winter session shows that unlike summer, most students are willing to work fewer hours. This can be attributed to a higher number of distractions during this time period.

Here is a summation of the points outlined above:

	Starts	Ends
Fall	Beginning of September	Mid-December
Winter	Mid-December	Mid-January
Spring	Mid-January	Beginning of May
Summer	Beginning of May	End of August

	Winter	Spring	Fall	Summer
PROS	Great opportunity for short-term special projects.	Second most common time students seek internships; tends to be a busier time in many organizations when projects need to be completed.	Tends to be a slower period in many industries, allowing staff to be more attentive.	Largest candidate pool; best opportunity for completing larger projects; Easier to provide a consistent program
CONS	Extremely brief period of time; competition with vacations and holiday season; much smaller candidate pool.	Competing with class time, homework, school activities, and possibly other jobs.	Same as spring. In addition, students are just returning from summer.	Requires the most structure and planning.

"NEITHER OF [MY INTERNSHIPS] were paid; at times, both organizations expected me to put the internship as a priority over my class work and familial responsibilities (as a student in an unpaid internship position!), especially the most recent one, which is why I gave it bad reviews. The most recent one tried to fail me when I wouldn't commit to more time than originally agreed upon, even when I explained to them that I could not due to schoolwork responsibilities."

"MAKE THE intern happy to walk in every day that they have to work. The work that should be required of an intern should be work that is enjoyable to complete and will teach valuable skills. Interns typically have a lot to do, especially during the school year, and it should not be a chore for the intern to complete unmanageable and inappropriate tasks."

"THE COMPANY respected the fact that I was a full time student and took that into consideration when making my schedule."

The Boss

Two key players from within your organization must commit fully to the internship program in order for its launching to succeed: the internship coordinator and supervisors. The internship coordinator does the legwork related to the internship program. He or she decides which departments receive interns, assigns supervisors, reviews intern work plans, writes job descriptions, conducts recruiting activities, and maintains the contact with universities that require organization follow-up.

Interns directly report to supervisors who establish their day-to-day activities and conduct evaluations of the interns' work when necessary. Depending on the size of your organization, you may find that you are playing the role of the coordinator and the supervisor. In larger organizations, however, supervisors (typically line managers) and the individual who coordinates the entire process (typically someone in Human Resources) are usually separate.

Work

Students expect a reasonable amount of work. In fact, they want it. In the student survey, 99% of students agreed that by the time they complete an internship program, they should be better prepared to work in that particular field. The level of preparation that a student ultimately gains from an internship is attributed mainly to the work that they fulfill.

> *"INTERNSHIPS NEED to ensure that students will receive the learning experience that they are looking for. There is nothing worse than saying that you interned somewhere and then have to explain that you just filed documents all summer. The intern needs to have something to take away from the experience, not just sore fingers or paper cuts."*
>
> *"I FEEL that internships expect too little from a participant and they get dragged down with menial tasks that provide little, if any, valuable work experience. On the other hand, I also feel like they can be on the exact opposite end- that certain programs expect too much from a participant; that they assign too much work or assign projects that are way over one's head. It is important to find a place or come to an understanding about a middle ground. A balance should be made between putting forth an effort and being involved in projects and tasks so that one feels useful and helpful; however, it should also be recognized that most internships are occurring while a student has an entire other life to worry about at the same time."*

> *"THEY SHOULD make sure that the intern feels as though they're an employee and not just some college kid that they can dump their dirty, boring paperwork on. A real part of the experience of an internship is to see what it would be like doing that job – not doing administrative work."*

Creating a Work Plan

Deciding specific assignments interns will complete during their tenure is one of the most important and delicate processes an organization will accomplish in regards to internship programming. Keep in mind that the top three reasons students pursue internships are educationally based – in other words, they want to learn. The Intern Work Plan details the projects that the interns will be completing and it helps to ensure that all activities contain some degree of learning. While clerical work in an internship is to be expected, this type of work should be kept to a minimum. However, even clerical work should be entered into the work plan. All proposed work for the intern should be in the work plan. The job description used for marketing the internship should be ultimately based on the Intern Work Plan.

> *"WHAT I liked best about my internship was the real-life work environment. My supervisor would give me certain tasks to complete and give dates and times when she would want them done by. I really appreciated how she treated me like a real employee and not 'just an intern.'"*

Short-Term vs. Long-Term Projects

From the research, it can be seen that there is a general disconnect between the amount of time that supervisors anticipate an assignment will take an intern to complete, and the actual time necessary for the intern to finish. Generally, *interns finish work much quicker than supervisors predict*. It is recommended that students be given mostly short-term projects (one hour to a few days turn around time) along with one or two long-term projects (due towards the end of the term).

> *"MY SUPERVISOR had very good insights but was often busy with work. I had to wait before finishing something because I had a lot of little questions to ask but he was often on the phone."*

With this format, students always have something to work on, even if the supervisor is unavailable to answer questions regarding a short-term project. This is considered a best practice. Students want to be useful, with 97% agreeing that they should be given enough work to be kept busy.

> *"I WOULD often do work faster than it would be assigned to me, so there was a good chunk of time I didn't have much to do."*
>
> *"SOME OF the projects were long and boring and sometimes my supervisor was too busy to give me something else to do when I was done with a project."*

Learning Objectives

The learning objective describes what you expect the intern to learn upon the successful completion of the activity. For example, suppose you host an intern in your organization's training department. A long-term project that the intern might complete is the creation of a training manual for a new e-learning software package. The learning objective might be to "develop e-learning skills." A short term project an intern might complete in the finance department is creating graphs based on daily sales levels. The learning objective here might be to "gain an understanding of sales reporting." Maybe the intern will have contact with industry professionals outside of your organization. The objective for this might be "enhance overall knowledge of the restaurant industry." As you can see, objectives can be either narrow or broad in focus, but nonetheless they should be clear to both the organization and the intern.

> *"I FELT as though there was not enough for me to do when my supervisor was away all day at meetings or conferences. Those days were relaxing but I wasn't there to relax, I was there to learn. "*

Learning Tasks

Learning tasks describe the "how" of an internship activity. They provide for a specific description of what the intern will do in order to accomplish the learning objective. A single learning objective may be accompanied by more than one learning task. Let's look back at the long-term project example mentioned above. A learning task associated with developing e-learning skills might be to "write a learning guide for employees." The learning task for achieving a greater depth in sales reporting might be to "produce daily sales reports with graphs." Lastly, a learning task for an intern working, meeting, or speaking with external industry professionals might be to "correspond with personnel within the restaurant industry."

Evaluation Methods

Evaluation methods describe how the supervisor will measure the output from the learning tasks, to explore if the learning objective has been reached. While there is a whole section in this publication providing suggestions on the topic of evaluating interns, it is important to note here that it is a critical, and often overlooked, responsibility of the organization. Evaluation methods may include a review by the supervisor (in person, on the phone, or through email), intern self-assessment, and/or gauging overall acceptance of the work by other employees in the organization. It is considered a best practice to provide evaluations in writing whenever possible so the student has something of record that they can show to their university and future employers.

You Already Have the "Meat"

Learning tasks are the "meat" to the "internship sandwich." They represent the work that interns will actually perform. You already determine tasks for part-time employees, full-time employees, and temporary employees, even if your organization doesn't refer to them as "learning tasks." One of the keys to a successful internship program is relating each and every proposed task into a learning objective that can be related to the intern and evaluated. It may be helpful to actually start in the middle (learning tasks) to determine objectives and evaluation methods.

Meaning of Menial Tasks

We have all heard of "menial tasks" and their impact on internship programs. When students and seasoned internship coordinators refer to menial tasks, they are referring to administrative work that does not provide the student with any educational benefit. Most of the time, the term directly refers to filing, stapling, collating, hanging flyers, etc. An important distinction is that interns expect menial tasks.

The trick is balancing the amount of menial tasks with the amount of genuine work, which leads to learning opportunities. Menial tasks can provide significant learning for students, but host sites tend to rush students through menial tasks, which eliminates any possible learning outcomes. By allowing students some extra time to absorb the information, menial tasks may become beneficial. Provide students with the big picture aspect and explain to them the importance of what they are doing.

> *"MY INTERNSHIP was an odd mix of both extremely interesting work about 5-10% of the time, and INCREDIBLY boring, menial work for the other 90-95%."*
>
> *"I LIKED the fact that I got experience within the field. I wasn't stuck making copies and getting coffee all the time (although I did have to do those things sometimes, as was expected.) I was improving my writing skills and getting a feel for what a public relations job would be like."*

Increased Experience Should Be Met with Increased Responsibility

As the internship experience progresses, students should have the opportunity to demonstrate an increased level of responsibility. This is a sign of good faith from the organization, in that they have confidence in the abilities of the student. Of the students who had participated in internships, 72% agreed or strongly agreed that they were able to assume additional responsibility as their level of experience increased.

> *"I WAS given the opportunity to prove myself. Initially they did not plan on me completing work similar to an Account Coordinator, seeing as I was hired as an intern; but they were impressed with my work and I was given the chance to complete more complicated projects once I proved myself."*

Don't Leave Things Out

It is an overall best practice in the Human Resources field to provide job candidates with a realistic preview of their potential job duties. It was once routine for recruiters to make jobs sound highly alluring and exciting. The candidate would accept a job offer only to be disappointed with their employment and leave the company prematurely, leading to a high turnover rate and high acquisition costs. In an internship program, a realistic job preview is just as, if not more, important. Students are present to learn more about a specific job in a particular industry, with the hopes of possibly being offered a full-time position. By hiding certain tasks of a particular job function, an organization can only harm their relationships with these potential full-time employees. Virtually all (98%) of students agreed that they must be given a realistic preview of the field during an internship program. Approximately 1 in every 5 interns reported that they only slightly agreed, or did not agree at all, that they were actually given this realistic preview.

> "WHAT I liked the most was that it was very hands on. I had goals and objectives to accomplish, my supervisor helped me to design the right kind of experiment, but I got to carry it out, and even learn the technique, on my own. In a way, that was very empowering."

Provide for Group Work

Interns place a great deal of value on feeling like they are a part of the organization, as opposed to just feeling like temps who do not belong. One opportunity to provide them with a more "at home" feeling is to assign them group work. Group work can be completed with other interns from within your organization or with employees that are working on similar projects. About 90% of students agreed that they should be given the opportunity to work in groups during an internship, while over half (54%) of interns surveyed disagreed or only slightly agreed that they were actually provided with group work.

Don't Be Afraid to Challenge Interns

Many organizations choose not to provide interns with challenging jobs, for two main reasons: the work that needs to be completed is by nature not challenging; or staff members lack faith in the ability of interns to effectively complete the work. However, the fact remains that 98% of students agree that the work completed should be challenging and stimulating, and 14% of interns felt that it was not. One component to ensuring that work is challenging is allowing interns the opportunity to work on a project from creation to completion.

Assist Interns with Setting Priorities

The vast majority of students (92%) agreed that they must be given the opportunity to set priorities. Of the interns surveyed, 86% agreed that they were actually given the opportunity to set priorities. The data suggests that while setting priorities is important to students, they may need some help. This can simply be done by supervisors suggesting to interns which projects need to be completed first.

> *"I REALLY liked the openness of the internship project. I was able to design my own program and carry it out with my own timeline/objectives, while still working closely with my supervisors."*

Providing for "Core Competencies"

The idea of core competencies as it relates to interns is that the students wish to build upon their existing skill sets during the internship experience. While much of what they will learn is work-related and industry/job-specific, there is something to be said about assisting interns in improving upon "core competency" skills such as writing, presenting, etc. When structuring an internship program, it is best to keep the core competency list on Page 59 in mind, and try to match as many competencies as possible with the activities and tasks that are planned. From the survey data, it is apparent that students who took part in an internship recognized that the experience helped them improve on all of the listed competencies and skills to some degree, with the only exception being reading and writing.

SURVEY DISCUSSION

Table C (on Page 59) shows the mean ranking of core competencies, based on students who had completed an internship, in order of most to least improved. Column A displays the rank and Column B presents the mean response (based on a 5 point scale) from the survey takers.

Table C		
A		**B**
1	Communicating	4.03
2	Listening	3.85
3	Taking Direction	3.85
4	Problem Solving	3.75
5	Decision Making	3.70
6	Critical Thinking	3.67
7	Teamwork	3.65
8	Networking	3.55
9	Leadership	3.44
10	Ethics	3.35
11	Presenting	3.14
12	Reading	2.99
13	Writing	2.98

A Long-Term Goal: Rotational Internships

One of the largest and most recent trends in internship programming is the idea of rotational internships. A rotational internship is one where the intern has the opportunity to experience work in either different areas of a specific discipline or, in very broad rotational programs, different areas of an entire company. The recent growth in rotational internships is directly related to their unique ability to provide students with the most workplace experience.

> *"IT WAS great to gain different views of the jobs within the organization (client relations, receptionist, inventory/ordering, maintenance, etc.)"*

A departmental rotational program would allow the intern to experience different areas of a department for a specific period of time. For example, a rotational internship program in an HR department may have the intern working three weeks in compensation, three weeks in recruiting, three weeks in benefits, and three weeks in training.

An agency-wide rotational program would have the intern working for a specific period of time in different function areas. For example, the intern might work three weeks in HR, three weeks in marketing, three weeks in accounting, and three weeks in legal.

The major advantage of a rotational program is that it guarantees that the intern will be exposed to as many people as possible within a department or an organization. If the main goal of your internship program is to potentially hire interns as full-time employees after they graduate, few models could be better than a rotational program.

> *"I WAS able to experience the company's atmosphere as a whole, because I was brought out into the field to work with other areas of the business. I enjoy working with people and my supervisor made sure I met almost everyone."*

However, rotational programs are not right for every organization. If you are just starting to implement an overall internship program or college relations plan, working with a rotational model is probably not the best choice. Gaining proficiency in a one-job internship model first will aid greatly in the proper implementation of a rotational program. The question of an organization's culture also comes into focus when dealing with a rotational program. Since the intern will be handed off several times between departments and supervisors, the chance for "hiccups" in the student's learning experience becomes greater. There is also a greater time commitment on the part of the internship coordinator to recruit four or five total supervisors per intern, as opposed to just one supervisor for the non-rotational program.

SUPERVISORS

As discussed in the earlier section regarding program structure, there are separate key individuals in the management process of an internship program: the internship coordinator and the internship supervisor. The internship supervisor is the individual from whom the intern receives job assignments, work-related feedback, and evaluations.

> *"I WANT an internship that will have a good supervisor willing to teach their interns everything they need to know and be willing to answer any questions they may have. I also want an internship that I learn something in and where I am able to use my skills that I have learned from my courses."*

If you were to perform an internet search for "best practices in internships" you would find a list of varying best practices from universities, associations, and some employers. However, the selection of a supervisor will most likely not be mentioned even once on the list. In almost all cases, the supervisor is the direct manager of the intern. The relationship is identical to the relationship between a manager and line employee; and the latest research shows that the way employees are treated by their manager is often the sole determinant in whether an organization retains that employee. The same applies in an internship.

Remember, interns are going to represent your organization. The supervisor has a great deal to do with whether the student will have a positive or negative influence on your campus recruiting strategies. Therefore, choosing and properly training a supervisor is an extremely important, yet currently under-appreciated, component to an internship program. So under-appreciated, in fact, that only 2% of organizations reported that the individual who is suggested to be the supervisor for interns is evaluated for their ability to act in a supervisory role for students. The vast majority (81%) of organizational survey respondents strongly disagreed, disagreed, or were neutral when asked if they evaluated potential internship supervisors. Choosing a supervisor, and evaluating that person for the ability to perform as an internship supervisor is an important step in the process that must not be overlooked.

Just over two-thirds of interns reported that their supervisor was involved in their internship. Almost 10% reported that their supervisor's involvement in the internship was minimal, if any. 69% of students agreed or strongly agreed that they would want their supervisor to be involved in the internship.

Interestingly, 27% of students were stuck in the middle and unsure if they would want their supervisor to be involved in the internship. This disconnect speaks loudly to students' expectations of supervisor involvement in internships. It is likely that these students have the expectation, based on the experiences of their peers and friends, that supervisors do not, and should not, have a strong involvement in the internship. Many students fail to realize the importance of the supervisor's role, as do many organizations.

A Cautionary Note

Because the process of choosing an intern's supervisor is delicate, this publication would be incomplete without making an important distinction. An individual who is an excellent supervisor of full-time, experienced individuals is not necessarily an effective internship supervisor. Providing supervision of a college student with little or no work experience is considerably different. Through our workshop presentations, we have had the chance to present best practices to audiences from both universities and organizations. The universities almost always recognize the difference, and the organizations almost always miss it. Thus, this is one of the largest gaps that requires special attention. Organizations need to evaluate their expectations and adjust them as appropriate.

SUPERVISOR SKILL SETS

The following are some skills that intern supervisors should possess to be as effective as possible.

Allow the Intern to Ask Questions, and then Be Sure to Answer Them

Interns, being brand new to an organization, will have several questions relating to work assignments, industry standards, and the organization itself. Keep in mind that one of the key reasons the student is working for the organization in the first place is to gain a deeper understanding of the industry and outfit. If they do not ask questions, they will not have that chance, which will ultimately lead to an unhappy intern. Equally as important is providing the intern with answers to their questions. This will ensure that they can properly do their job and that they are being provided an educationally sound experience.

Of the 1,596 students who participated in an internship, 81% agreed or strongly agreed that they were given the opportunity to ask questions of their supervisor. However, 38 of these same students did not agree that they were given the chance to have their questions answered. In total, 253 did not agree that they were given the opportunity to even ask questions and 291 did not agree that their questions were given satisfactory answers.

> *"MY SUPERVISOR was excellent! He always made sure I knew what I was doing, never thought any question was stupid, and always treated me with respect."*
>
> *"WHAT I liked best about my internship was that once I had been given proper instructions on what to do, I was set free to do work on my own with little supervision. I felt as though I had gained the trust and respect of my supervisor, and he always seemed pleased."*
>
> *"WHAT I liked best about my internship was how my supervisor made it her priority to find time to help me with any questions or problems that may have been an obstacle for me to overcome."*
>
> *"IT WAS a laid back environment. My supervisor was very accessible to me and eager to answer any questions I had about the organization or my tasks."*

Be Available for Consultation

Being available for consultation is similar to being available for questions, the only difference being that a consultation tends to take a bit more time. While a question may only take 30 seconds to answer, a consultation is a more informative conversation. There is a great opportunity to provide the intern with valuable knowledge when consulting with them. An effective consultation will allow the intern to be better at their jobs. It will allow them to continue their assigned work in a more efficient manner.

> *"MY ADVISOR was disorganized and, after assigning me over 2,500 contracts to go through, disappeared for the duration of the internship."*

Three quarters of interns agreed or strongly agreed that their supervisor was available for consultation, while 7% of interns strongly disagreed or disagreed with the same statement. Not surprisingly, 98% of students strongly agreed, agreed, or somewhat agreed that they would want their supervisors to be available for a consultation, should they take part in an internship program.

This does not mean that the supervisor needs to be available for the intern whenever the intern requests attention. It does, however, stress the importance of having both long-term and short-term projects. What this does mean is that the supervisor needs to respond to the intern in a timely manner. If the supervisor cannot consult with the intern he or she should remind the student that they can work on other projects in the meantime.

> *"MY SUPERVISOR was horrible. She was not present physically 70% of the time, so I would have no direction."*

> *"MY SUPERVISOR was based out of Paris, so we only got to see him for four days over the course of five weeks. "*

Supervisors Must also Be Instructors

As with any other managerial role, the supervisor must not only provide the intern with work, but also explain in detail what they are expecting the intern to actually accomplish. If the supervisor simply hands the intern an assignment, or emails it with little description, the intern will not be able to complete the work. By providing the intern with outcome expectations, the supervisor can be assured that the intern will be on the right track when completing the assignment. It is in this role that the supervisor is also acting as an instructor.

> *"I WASN'T given enough guidance. I was thrown into the sales world with no experience and asked to sell a product I understood very little about."*

The data suggests that supervisors may need assistance being effective instructors. In response to the question "is being given adequate explanation concerning assigned tasks of importance?" the mean response (on a 5 scale) from students was 4.16, as opposed to interns whose mean response was a 3.86. Students expect far more explanation to be given than what is currently being provided for.

> *"I THINK the key is to have a well-structured program with an enthusiastic supervisor that possesses strong communication skills."*

A closer look at the data shows that 68% of interns report that they agree or strongly agree that they were given adequate explanation. A striking 83% of students agree or strongly agree that they should be given adequate explanation.

Treat the Intern Professionally and Respectfully

Interns are employees of the organizations for which they work. It is critically important to understand that the way interns are treated reflects on the overall organization. Interns who are treated poorly by their supervisor will believe that the organization is an undesirable place to work.

Approximately 13% of interns strongly disagreed, disagreed, or only partially agreed that their supervisor treated them respectfully during the internship program. About 16% of interns felt the same way when asked if their supervisor treated them professionally. While the percentages are low, they represent over 450 students who were not treated with a reasonable degree of respect. Being that this is easily correctible by the organization, it is highly recommended that a supervisor is chosen who will treat interns with the professionalism and respect any employee or contractor of the organization deserves.

> *"IT'S NOT necessary to hold the intern's hand, but that doesn't mean they don't require some supervision. Many employers don't understand the difference, and that's important."*
>
> *"MY DIRECT supervisor was not respectful and offered no opportunities for personal growth during the internship."*
>
> *"I UNFORTUNATELY did not get the respect I believed I deserved from my supervisor. He did not treat me like an employee and made inappropriate comments. Other than that, I was treated great by the other employees and felt welcomed by them."*
>
> *"I REALLY enjoyed working with the amazing people that I did. They treated me very professionally and allowed me to take on genuine responsibilities."*

Supervisors Should Be Approachable Individuals

Aside from a possible mentor, the supervisor is typically the interns' only contact within the organization that they will have a significant relationship with. If the intern is having a problem, whether it is related to a work assignment or another employee, it is likely that the intern will want to approach their supervisor regarding the situation. If the supervisor is an unapproachable individual, the intern will hold back, which would be detrimental to their internship experience. More than three quarters of intern respondents (77%) agreed or strongly agreed that they did feel comfortable talking to their supervisor regarding problems they had encountered.

> *"MY BOSS ... would tell us to do something, we'd do it, then she'd change her mind and do everything over the way she wanted it, usually throwing out everything we did. It made us feel terrible. We put so much effort into all the projects and she'd throw them away in seconds without even consulting us. She was also very disrespectful when someone's personal opinion differed from her own. At one point she singled me out about a certain issue and sent me more than 10 emails a day trying to 'educate' me."*
>
> *"I REALLY enjoyed the professional relationship I had with my supervisor. She was reliable, open, and understanding. It made working at the internship easier to adjust."*
>
> *"MY SUPERVISOR was a very good mentor and friend towards me. I did not feel out of place or unable to talk about a problem."*

MARKETING

Targeting Universities

Before an organization can begin marketing the internship program to universities (and their students), a decision must be made as to which universities will be targeted. It is important to note that every university is different. The best method for targeting universities is to get to know the ones in your area.

Some questions that you should consider are:
- What makes each university unique?
- What degree programs does the university offer?
- What resources are available within the institution to support the students taking part in the degree programs that you will be recruiting from?
- Does the university have any sort of research center dedicated to any of its degree programs?
- Is it easy to find information about how the university interacts with employers?

Granted, learning details about all of the universities in a region can be difficult, if not nearly impossible. For example, there are over 100 colleges in the Greater Boston area. It would take weeks, if not months or even years to learn all of the pertinent information about every university, so pick a few to start with, then grow from there.

Identify Universities by Specific Degree Programs

Another approach is to visit the website for The College Board. You may recognize the name if you know of high school students that have recently taken the PSAT/NMSQT and the SAT. The College Board, based in New York City, is the educational testing organization in charge of the college admissions test. Over the past several years, the College Board has also begun offering a resource to its website visitors. The "college search" portion of the website allows individuals to perform a college search based on specific search criteria including geographic area, student clubs offered, financial information, and average test scores. While the website is geared specifically to help high school students target universities where they wish to apply, it is also a tremendous resource for you to target universities for your internship program.

To use this method, first see **Appendix A** in this publication. This is a list of the degree programs that the College Board has available on their website. You will notice that the list is extremely specific. This should help weed out the universities that might not be best for your internship program. Make a list of the degree programs that you would like to target. (You may perform several searches if your internship program involves positions that are vastly different from each other – for example a position in marketing and a position in engineering.)

Visit www.CollegeBoard.com and find the link for the "College Match-Maker" (At the time this publication went to print, it could be found on the left hand side of the home page.) Once you click the link, you will be in the College MatchMaker interface. You don't want your search to be too specific, because you want to receive a good number of candidate schools.

At the top of the interface, click "location." Select the states where you would like the university to be located. Then click "Majors and Academics." Using the list in Appendix A, you can search for specific degree programs. By clicking on "show results" a list will be generated with all of the colleges that fit your criteria.

You can get as specific as you would like with the search criteria to generate different results. Once you are satisfied with the search results, you now have your list of colleges to target for the program.

Do Not Choose Only "Feeder Schools"

Intern Bridge recently worked with an organization that had just been acquired, and the new CEO was determined to implement an internship program – something that had never been done before in this large organization. In speaking with the HR staff about the best way to implement their program, one of the high-level HR partners made the comment that when he first started working for the organization several years before, the culture was to do their very best to obtain MBA applicants from the top business schools for all of their positions. He jokingly remarked that even the mailroom worker had an MBA.

This mentality represents one of the largest gaps in employing graduates of the United States higher education system. Employers typically reach out to the "big name" schools that achieve high rankings, and the schools without the brand name tend to lose out. When you seriously think about this, it doesn't make sense. Once an entry-level employee enters an organization, they become just that – an entry level employee at the bottom of the organizational totem pole. At the entry level, someone from a "brand name" school and someone from a "no name" school will most likely end up working next to each other, performing the same tasks.

Are all colleges and universities created equal? Of course not. But to only recruit interns from the popular schools would be making a serious mistake. Your organization will ultimately lose out on highly qualified candidates and the chance to increase diversity within your internship program and organization. Further, the brand name schools do not usually have a problem with attracting organizations to recruit their students – the employers are always knocking at these colleges' doors. Their students are saturated with options. The "no name" schools often have to go out and recruit organizations to come to their campus. If you recruit at these schools, you will have less competition for students that can do fantastic work.

Transportation Issues

It is important to keep in mind that not all students have access to vehicles. Many colleges (especially those in urban settings) prohibit some, if not all, students from bringing a car to campus. This needs to be a consideration when planning which universities you will target. It may be advantageous to target the schools closest to your organization.

WORKING WITH UNIVERSITIES

Time-consuming, yet Critical!

Marketing your available internship program to students at specific universities will require the most time on your part. The process works something like this:

Step 1: Contact the college career office and determine who is in charge of internships.

Step 2: Contact the internship coordinator to open a dialogue about your internship program.

Step 3: Submit your preformatted job description OR complete the college's detailed internship form.

Step 4: Select a date and time to conduct interviews (possibly on-campus).

Step 5: Review cover letters and resumes from applicants.

Step 6: Conduct interviews (possibly on-campus).

Although this process seems simple, you must understand that you will have to go through the same process for every college that you choose to target! For the most part, you will have to post the position with the college even if you plan on recruiting interns through methods other than the campus career development office. If you plan on having multiple rounds of interviews, it is common for the first round to take place on-campus or over the phone, and for the second round to take place at the host site.

How Closely Does My Organization Have to Work with Colleges?

The answer to this question depends on the college you are contacting. Different colleges have different standards for their internship programs. Almost every college you contact will require that some legwork is completed before the internship is posted to their students; it's just a matter of how detailed and time-consuming the process is.

Some colleges will just have you fax or email a copy of the internal job description, and then they will do the rest of the marketing and scheduling work. Other colleges will require that you not only complete one of their internal forms, but also that you arrange a meeting with someone from their career office who will come on-site and inspect the space where the intern will be working.

The college has a particular interest in ensuring that the intern will remain safe at all times while taking part in an internship experience. Therefore, you must be flexible when working with the college. Depending on the institution that you target and the brand of your organization, the college may not find it worth their time to negotiate their process with you. As harsh as this might sound, it is a reality. For the most part, the colleges hold the golden key to potential intern candidates and you must adhere to their guidelines for your program to be a complete success.

Further, do not expect the university to do the legwork for you. Organizations often have the misconception that universities will offer a "matching service," and that it will be done on a moment's notice. This is not the job of the university; there are very few, if any, that actually offer this type of service. Universities will help you develop job descriptions and discuss your program with you, but do not expect them to recommend specific students. The role of match-making is up to you, and it will allow you to make informed decisions leading to a mutually beneficial experience.

Collaboration Plague

An organization decides to host interns. They contact a local university for advice on how to reach out to their student population. The organization is greeted excitedly by the college. However, the college has several guidelines that they wish the organization to follow before they are able to market the position to students. The organization, unable or unwilling to abide by the guidelines, decides not to target the university for their internship program.

This has been affectionately named "collaboration plague" by Intern Bridge. Across the country, universities and organizations are trying to collaborate on the "ideal" internship program. Organizations want more flexibility, whereas the universities insist on a rigid program with a high degree of supervision. The interests of the two groups are common, but not necessarily equally weighted. Unfortunately, it is the students who suffer, because internship programs in some cases simply don't happen, or operate at a level of unrealized potential.

The truth is that total 100% agreement is often difficult (while not entirely impossible.) This is, of course, not meant to discourage you, but rather to reiterate that you should expect the universities you contact to have procedures and requirements that your organization will need to fulfill before they will allow the position to be posted to students.

SURVEY DISCUSSION

Table D represents how intern respondents learned about their opportunities.

Column A reflects the ranked responses of how interns learned about the opportunity.

Column B represents the matching response from students who have not taken part in an internship experience.

A	Table D	B
1	Friend or family contact	1
2	Personal contact	2
3	Campus Career Development Office or Field Placement Office	6
4	Faculty contact	3
5	Organization website	10
6	Online career directory (Monster.com, etc.)	14
7	Campus internship information session	5
8	Fellow student who was a past or current intern with the organization	4
9	Fellow student	9
10	Career fair	8
11	Student organization	12
12	Internship fair	7
13	Advertisement in print	13
14	Organization open house	11

Table E shows which resources organizations who host interns find most useful.

Column A represents the ranked responses of methods organizations use to market their opportunity.

Table E	
A	
1	Working with the career development office at local colleges
2	Word of mouth from past or current interns
3	Faculty contacts at local colleges
4	Organization website
5	College campus internship information sessions
6	Career fairs
7	Outreaching to student clubs on local college campuses
8	Internship fairs
9	Commercial career websites (such as Monster.com)
10	Hosting an open house
11	Direct email marketing
12	Advertisement in print

Utilizing the Campus Career Center

As previously discussed, the campus career center is a great resource, and in most cases, a mandatory one. Employers ranked using the career development office most effective when trying to recruit interns for the program. A glimpse at student responses shows that both students who have had an internship, and those that have not, did not use the campus career office as their primary point of contact.

A bit of caution as we move forward.

The ranked data is based on the feedback from students at all 31 colleges where the survey was implemented. It is important to note that while the overall ranks are important, each college's career office operates differently. In some universities, the career office is an integral part of the student experience. Students may be required to meet with a representative from the career office before they can even post their resume to employers. At other institutions, however, the career office may have a less prominent place in the community and have less contact with students.

There are several colleges where the career office is staffed by just one person who is in charge of full-time recruiting, internships, career advising, and student workshops. At colleges such as these, where the career office is a less centralized unit of the college community, students may seek one of the alternate sources listed above. It is always a good practice to work with the university career office, in addition to other methods you decide to pursue.

Power of Networking

Interestingly, both students and interns found great value in tapping into their network to pursue an internship. Whether it was a friend, family member, or a personal or faculty contact, students found that networking with these individuals was more beneficial than seeking an internship through a source such as a campus career center. On the other hand, organizations resorted to the traditional method of contacting the career office as their main point of entry into the college. The internship program should be marketed internally so employees are empowered to share information with potential intern candidates. While organizations should certainly continue to work closely with the college career office, you should also have an understanding that, depending on the size of your organization, effectively marketing an internship may be as simple as broadcasting an internal email.

Faculty Contacts

Faculty members of a university are an incredible resource. Not only do they typically teach in a specific discipline, but they also have been exposed to a large part of the student body and are familiar with students' strengths and weaknesses. These individuals can help identify great candidates for your internship program. Students often turn to faculty members when they are seeking an internship. Students assume that faculty are a part of large industry-related networks and have several contacts that can lead to an internship offer (which is usually a reality.)

The challenge can be getting in touch with faculty. Some colleges make it easier than others. If you visit the university website, you may find a "faculty search" option that will let you search for faculty members based on the disciplines they teach. You can contact the person via email or telephone (some websites will only provide you with the extension number and no email address.) You may need to be aggressive with follow-ups as faculty members are usually very busy individuals with multiple projects and classes on their plates. Faculty want what is best for their students, so if you have a quality opportunity to offer they will contact you and at least point you in the right direction.

For colleges that do not provide an online directory, call the main college number and ask who the Department Chair is for the specific discipline you are looking for (for example, the Accounting Department Chair or the Engineering Department Chair.) The position of Department Chair is typically only given to faculty members who have been members of the college community for a considerable amount of time. The Chair should be able to recommend a faculty contact (if not themselves) and possibly students as well. Don't be afraid to ask if the Chair or faculty member would forward an email message from you to the students in their classes or in other classes studying the same discipline.

Empowering Full-Time Employees to Help

Again, empower your employees to recommend family members and young people they may know. Allowing employees to help with the process may open the doors to connections at local universities. To help lighten the load, you may wish to ask full-time employees if they would be in charge of researching candidates from their alma mater. An employee who graduated from ABC University would know how the system works at that particular school. They may also know, and have strong relationships with, specific faculty members and administrators who can help single out students.

Get on Campus

One of the best things you can do to promote your internship program to students is to increase the awareness of your brand on the campuses you target. For instance, you can have former interns act as ambassadors to faculty and students. However, this may be a lengthy process quality-control-wise, and really requires that your organization recruits more than just one intern every term. It is suggested, rather, that your organization send other recruiters to get on campus.

Sponsor an Information Session

When you decide to recruit interns at ABC University, you have the option of contacting the career center to post the internship and then sitting back and hoping that the resumes, cover letters, and applications come piling in. This is most likely not a realistic expectation. One of the best ways to get on campus is to sponsor an information session, which many college campuses will help you to plan. The sessions, which usually take place in the evening, will be marketed to the student body through the career office. Even if a student is unable to attend the program due to prior obligations, seeing your organizations name in campus-wide email or on flyers will increase brand awareness. Furthermore, students who do attend the program will receive a great deal of information about your organization and internship opportunities, thus increasing the number of qualified applicants.

Be sure to ask colleges whether or not they require students to attend your information session prior to interviewing with you. This will allow you to cater your presentation in regards to how detailed you want to be about the specific job, or if you want to give a wider company overview. Of course, if candidates will be interviewing the next day, you want to focus more on the job that interests them, while a more general presentation can be given for non-applicants who just want to learn more about the company.

Get Out to Fairs, Time Permitting

Most colleges host a job fair for either their specific school, or for a group of schools through a consortium effort. For a long time, these fairs have been focused on the full-time recruiting of graduating seniors. A recent trend is a completely separate fair geared specifically for internships. These "internship fairs" follow the same model as the full-time fairs. Employers set up booths, hand out promotional items and business cards, and try to portray a positive image to students. In most cases, there are fees associated with exhibiting at internship fairs, but the fees are nominal.

There may be a substantial time commitment, however, depending on how many universities you choose to target for internship fairs.

Sponsor Student Organization Events

Sponsoring an event that is organized by a student club or organization can bolster brand awareness as well. Students tend to form clubs around the same disciplines that you are recruiting. Contact the college's Campus Life or Student Activities office for a complete list of clubs. You may wish to contact a student officer, as opposed to the advisor, who is typically a faculty member. Faculty advisors are usually also professors with a multitude of other responsibilities. While any type of sponsorship is subject to the advisor's approval, you should try to make a student officer a primary contact.

If you do not wish to increase expenses by monetarily sponsoring an event, you can also volunteer some time to the organization as a guest speaker. Many student clubs offer career exploration seminars in the evening where they invite guest speakers from a specific industry. Becoming a guest speaker will give students the opportunity to learn more about your industry, organization, and available intern positions.

For a sample list of student organizations, refer to **Appendix B**.

Application Process

Depending on the number of schools you decide to target and the popularity of the internship's discipline, you could receive hundreds of applications for each position. Be sure to acknowledge the receipt of each application, with a specific contact person. Students are persistent. They will follow-up with you repeatedly until you answer. For those candidates who do not receive an interview, be sure to email them explaining that at this time you don't believe they would be a fit for your organization but that you will keep their resume on file.

INTERVIEWING AND SELECTION

Interviewing your intern candidates is an important step that, surprisingly, some organizations skip. If you choose not to interview candidates, you will not truly know if they are a good fit for your program. Having an effective interview process is critical, and it needs to be treated professionally.

One of our placement students recently told us a story about a time she applied to work for a nationwide restaurant organization. The company had been to the job fair on campus. The job fair booth was tended by the manager of the local establishment in Boston, but if students were interested in applying, they had to contact someone else, whose business card was available. The company offered an in-depth management training program, part of which included time spent in the Wine Country of California. She eagerly applied.

She never received acknowledgement that her resume and cover letter had been received. Two weeks later, the recruitment manager emailed her to setup an interview time. When she called him at their scheduled time, the call went to voicemail. He returned the call the next day at a random time and expected her to be ready for the interview without notice. Luckily, she was. He was traveling and conducting the interview over his cell phone. The reception was lousy. About ten minutes into the interview he had to disconnect to go through airport security. He promised he would call back in a couple of minutes, but he did not call back for a half hour. The interview continued, on his cell phone, with the noise of airport announcements and travelers talking in the background. She also stated that the interviewer didn't take a genuine interest in anything about her – her educational experiences, leadership experiences, etc. All he asked was "what do you know about us" and "what would make you a good fit to work for us."

To make a long story short, she wasn't offered a position. But she also stated that even if she had been offered a position, she was so dissatisfied with the lack of professionalism from the interviewer that she wouldn't have accepted anyway. And, to further speak to our point that students are representatives no matter what (even at an early stage, such as an interview), she did tell all of her friends about her experience.

The point we are making with the previous story is not that students will be offended by phone interviews (in many cases, students prefer them, as it is less of a time commitment), but that you must treat the interview process as you would treat it for a full-time candidate – professionally and respectfully.

BEHAVIORAL INTERVIEWING

Important for Interviewing Intern Candidates

Behavioral interviewing in the internship setting is important for several reasons. First and foremost, it has become a customary and well-respected best practice for interviewing. Its advantages are numerous. Behavioral interviewing provides the means for employers to gain an honest glimpse into the potential of a job candidate.

From the college side, students are being coached by their career offices about the prevalence of behavioral interviews. Many students take part in mandatory education programs geared toward teaching them how to analyze a behavioral interview question and apply techniques to best answer the question. They participate in student-to-student mock interviews, and many universities tap into their alumni pool for special student-to-employer practice scenarios.

The bottom line is that students are going to enter an interview with the high expectation of being asked behavioral questions. Their judgment of the internship opportunity may become skewed if their expectation of the interview is not met. In the research, the vast majority of organizations responded that they ask behavioral questions of intern candidates during the interview process.

The Basics

The basic idea behind behavioral interviewing is that past performance is the best predictor of future behavior. For years, HR professionals asked candidates questions such as "what are your strengths?" or "what is your weakness?" And, for years, they received the same generic answers: "I'm a team player" or "I can't say no." Behavioral interviewing demands that the candidate provide examples of past behaviors to substantiate their claims. Using the examples above, a behavioral interviewer may ask the candidate to describe a time when they used their skills as a team player to achieve a goal, or to describe a time when the candidate didn't say no, and the outcome of a project that suffered as a result. Students are often taught the STAR method of how to respond to a behavioral interview question. The STAR method lays the groundwork for students to discuss the Situation they were in, the Task that needed to be completed, the Action they took to complete the task, and the Result they attained.

Interviewing a Student

The steps taken to interview students are similar to that of a full-time, experienced hire. One important difference to keep in mind is that when you are interviewing a college student, it could very well be their first job interview ever. That might change the dynamic of the interview a bit, and it may require that your questions be more probing in nature.

Step 1: Build Rapport

Building rapport with the candidate is important in any interview, but especially when working with college students. This is your chance to give the student a feeling of calm so that they will open up to you. Remember, the purpose of the interview is to determine if the student is a good fit for the organization. Presumably, you have already decided based on their cover letter and resume that they have the necessary skill set. Making small talk will give you the opportunity to learn more about the candidates past behaviors, and it may provide you with a basis to ask questions you may not have considered prior to the interview.

Step 2: Explain Note-Taking

If it is the student's first interview, you may create an increased level of anxiety as you frequently pause to take notes. The student may become confused, and think that they are performing poorly. It is important to briefly explain that taking notes is a necessary part of how you remember the qualifications of a candidate.

Step 3: Ask About Past Experiences

In a standard interview, this step would most likely read, "ask about past employment." However, depending on where the students are in their education, they may not have an extensive job history, or one that connects with the internship. On the flip side, they will most likely have taken part in unique experiences as part of their college experience. If it appears on their resume, it is what the student is most proud of in terms of non-classroom experience. Be sure to ask questions about it.

Step 4: Ask if the Student Has Any Questions

Students are coached by career departments to make sure they investigate an organization (via their website, news articles, etc.) before they go for an interview. They are also coached to have at least one question ready for the interviewer. Chances are that if the student has a genuine interest in the opportunity, they will have at least one question based solely on information learned in the interview process.

Step 5: Close the Interview

Thank the student for their interest in the position. It is in your best interest to give the student a timeline of when they will hear from you regarding a decision. Today's students are very persistent. Without a timeline, you will probably hear from the student several times per week until they are given a definitive answer.

Step 6: Send a Thank You

This is one trick that could set your opportunity apart from the rest. You may expect to receive a thank you note from the applicant; but what is rare, however, is the employer sending a thank you note. This is a great opportunity for you to reiterate the details of the position, thank the student for their interest, and remind them of when they are likely to hear a decision.

Please refer to **Appendix C** for a list of sample questions.

SELECTION

Now that the interviews are complete, it is time to select which candidates will become part of your internship program.

Create a Selection Strategy
The first step in selecting the interns for your program is to create a strategy. The main goal of creating a selection strategy is to ensure that you are being consistent with the applicants that are extended offers of employment. Before proceeding, create a list of specific criteria that you are looking for each candidate to possess. Then grade each remaining candidate on a rubric.

Background Checks
Depending on your organization, it may be a requirement that certain background checks be conducted on all of your potential employees. If that is the case, the policy most likely will lead to background checks having to be conducted for interns.

Type of Check	Number of Organizations
Reference Check	107
College Enrollment Confirmation	79
Criminal / CORI	70
Job History Confirmation	62
College Transcript	36
Drug Screening	29
Credit Check	16

College Enrollment and Transcript Confirmations
Verifications that are completed through the college take time. It would work better with the recruiting timeline if you have all applicants request enrollment and transcription verifications when they apply to your organization. Most colleges require that the request come from the student, especially transcripts, and under the Department of Education's Family Educational Rights and Privacy Act (FERPA), universities are not permitted to release transcripts without the consent of the student. The school, however, is permitted to release enrollment verification without permission. It will take a significant amount of time on your part to call each Registrar's office for every candidate to confirm enrollment or transcripts. It is best to notify students that this will be required as a part of the application process.

Note: College transcripts will come in an envelope with some sort of official seal. You should not accept transcripts which students print from their computers.

Selection Criteria

You should have some idea of how you will be picking interns before the selection process begins. By having this idea in mind before the selection process starts, you will minimize the likelihood of going with a "gut feeling" and maximize the opportunity to select fantastic interns.

Table F shows how employers rank each criterion according to most used in the selection of interns.

Table F	
1	Interview
2	People skills
3	Availability
4	Technical skills
5	Student's major
6	Level of education
7	Job experience
8	Recommendation(s) from professors
9	Recommendation(s) from previous employers
10	Grades
11	Volunteer experience
12	Student's expectations of monetary compensation

Student Availability

It is important to make clear during the interview process what your expectations are in terms of the level of commitment from the student. If your internship is in the fall or spring, then the internship will not be the top priority of the student (and you cannot expect it to be while classes are in session.) However, you need to make it clear that even though classes are in session, there is still an expectation that the student will create a schedule and stick to it except in cases of emergencies. Be sure to explain that an emergency is not a mid-term exam or a paper since, in almost all cases, they are given ample notice from their professors.

Since the student's availability is one of the topics you should be covering in an interview, you will have a good basis to see if the student is too overextended with other responsibilities (class, students clubs, etc.) to dedicate the amount of time that you feel is necessary. The student's availability should be a key factor in the selection process, as issues that arise during the internship pertaining to the student's schedule can become messy. It is best to figure out availability before the start of the program. If you are unsure that the student will have satisfactory availability, it is best to hire a different candidate.

ON-BOARDING

Only 56% of interns agreed or strongly agreed that they were satisfied with the quality of the orientation that they received, and only 43% of organizations agreed that the quality of the orientation they received was high.

On-boarding, or orientation, is your chance to show off your organization and prepare students for their internship experience. It serves a multitude of purposes. First, it provides the student with a chance to relieve some anxiety: few things can be more stressful for 20-year-old students than being placed in an environment with individuals older than they are who have been working with the organization or within the industry for several years. Without the on-boarding process, supervisors would be responsible for all of the topics covered within the program. Therefore, the process can save time for the intern's supervisors.

> **"SUPERVISORS CAN make one feel welcome from the start.
> I think a great start would lead to a great finish."**

The on-boarding program also helps to set realistic expectations for the intern. Remember that many students have had part-time jobs in the past to finance their education or social lives, but this doesn't mean that they are familiar with other aspects such as organizational culture and politics, the need for confidentiality, or other items specific to your organization. Organizations must be committed to the on-boarding process, including supervisors, who need to provide students with concentrated time at the beginning of the program. This level of direct supervision will decrease as interns become more independent and productive colleagues.

> **"THE MOST important thing an organization can do to make the internship
> experience meaningful is to train the person well and allow them to
> explore the field they are interested in."**

What to Include
Most organizations already have some sort of orientation in place for their new hires, and with a few tweaks, these are usually sufficient for an internship.

Some important items to include especially, for an internship orientation, are industry language that the student may not know on their own, acceptable dress for your organization's workplace, confidentiality issues, who the intern can go to with problems, if overtime is acceptable, and how to fill out timesheets.

One of the most beneficial pieces of information you can provide an intern is an organizational chart. Often an intern will be meeting with their supervisor when a colleague interrupts the meeting. By providing the intern with an organizational chart, the student can then go back to his or her desk and use the chart to see where that person works and what his or her position is. Having access to the chart is a great way to help interns become acclimated to the people within your organization.

Do Not Just Orient Students

If you are moving ahead with the internship program, then hopefully you have the support of the executive level personnel within your organization. However, most organizations do not currently provide any sort of employee orientation as it relates to the internship program. In fact, only 29% of employers agreed or strongly agreed that the quality of how employees are oriented about the internship program was high.

> "IN ORDER to make an internship experience meaningful an organization must be happy to have the intern there. It is obvious when someone is not wanted, and that causes uncomfortable feelings. Employees of the organization must be willing to tell the student all that they know and have learned from working in the environment and the student must also have some responsibility so that in the end he or she can feel as if something was accomplished."

Introduce Students to Employees

63% of interns reported that they agreed or strongly agreed that they were given a good introduction to the other employees when they first started the internship. It is incredibly important to make the intern feel welcome. There is no better way to do this than to provide the intern with a chance to meet employees, especially employees who work within the same department as the intern. One way to encourage introductions is to post interns' names, pictures, and bios on your organization's intranet. An employee with similar interests, or one who graduated from the same university, might reach out to the intern and make them feel welcome.

> *"AN ORGANIZATION can put more stress on internship programs and educate employees that such a program is an important part of the interns' experience and the company's image. They should also have well-planned tasks to help the intern gain experience as they work for the firm and promote a comfortable environment for the intern."*
>
> *"I TRIED to get an array of opportunities so that I was not only getting experience in one area. The best internships were ones that took me seriously, as a valuable asset to the organization with a distinct perspective."*
>
> *"IT WAS upsetting that sometimes I wasn't taken seriously by other employees. I was looked at as just an intern."*

Opportunity to Set Expectations

63% of interns reported that the organization's expectations of them were clear when they began their internship. The on-boarding process is the perfect time to set forth expectations. These expectations include everything from the intern's availability, to expectations for dress code and professional conduct.

If your organization has an internship coordinator in addition to separate supervisors, you most likely need to have two orientation programs. The first program would be for all of the interns. At this program, you would gather all of the interns together and provide them with information about your organization. The second orientation is intern-specific, and is individualized time that the intern will spend with the supervisors. This is the time when the supervisors need to lay out what activities and projects the intern will be involved in. Only 54% of interns reported that the activities or projects of their internship were made clear to them from the start. Be sure that interns have written goals.

> *"HAVE THE purpose and goals of the internship noted and reviewed to ensure each student completes those goals."*
>
> *"I WAS given a work load larger then I originally was lead to believe at the beginning of the internship."*
>
> *"I THINK the orientation describing my exact job description could have been better. "*

> *"I DIDN'T like the pacing of my internship; at first, we got off to a slow start, barely getting anything accomplished. Then, toward the end of the second week, my boss turned up the tempo and decided that we had to get X, Y, and Z done. Almost unrealistic in its nature, the timeline he had laid out in his head was undisclosed to me, so I had a difficult time imagining a) what his final goals were, b) how he wanted me to complete those goals, and c) how long he expected it to take me. I didn't like the complete lack of structure/training."*

> *"EACH INTERN worked for a specific researcher and I felt that mine was not specific enough when she explained my tasks. She expected me to learn how to use a complicated computer program in a few weeks which she herself didn't even understand. When I wasn't successful she was very disappointed and I was left feeling very frustrated. Also, we were to complete our own personal projects during that time as well, but it was difficult to balance the time."*

Beyond the Ordinary Presentation

Here is a list of some things you can do for interns to make them feel welcome beyond the informational presentation:

- Ask the Vice President of the division where the intern is working, or even the CEO, to stop by the interns' work space and personally welcome them. The brief greeting should only take a couple of minutes.
- Create a "Welcome Fall/Spring/Summer Interns" banner and display it somewhere the interns and full-time employees will see it.

> *"MY ORIENTATION was horrible, especially because the first week was really confusing and discouraging."*

Think Twice About "Childish" Icebreakers

A keystone of many orientation programs is to have employees take part in icebreaking activities. These activities, while they are effective at building morale and friendships, tend to be childish. The problem with having interns take part in such programs is that their goal is to enter an organization and be taken seriously as a professional. These icebreaking activities may make them feel that they are being patronized. This is not to say that icebreakers should not be conducted, but the ones that are chosen should be as professional as possible.

"*MAKE AN intern feel welcome, but not uncomfortable by treating them like a child. Give them appropriate work and allow for feedback in both directions.*"

YOU HAVE REACHED A HIDDEN GEM IN TOTAL INTERNSHIP MANAGEMENT

ON PAGE 90 AND 91, YOU WILL FIND A PARTIAL LIST OF STUDENT RESPONSES TO THE QUESTION OF:

"DESCRIBE YOUR INTERNSHIP EXPERIENCE WITH JUST ONE WORD."

THE WORDS, BOTH POSITIVE AND NEGATIVE IN NATURE FURTHER PROVE THAT YOUR ORGANIZATION MUST TAKE THE APPROPRIATE STEPS WHEN MANAGING AN INTERNSHIP PROGRAM!

Acceptable ◆ *Accomplished* ◆ Adaptable ◆ *Adequate* ◆ Advancing ◆

Authentic ◆ *Average* ◆ Awesome ◆ *Bad* ◆ Beautiful ◆ *Beneficial* ◆ B

Chaotic ◆ Chill ◆ *Confusing* ◆ Connective ◆ *Constructive* ◆ Consu

Determination ◆ *Developmental* ◆ Different ◆ *Difficult* ◆ Disappointi

Dynamite ◆ *Easy* ◆ Eclectic ◆ *Educational* ◆ Edutainment ◆ *E*

Enlightening ◆ Entertaining ◆ *Equipping* ◆ Essential ◆ *Eventful* ◆

Exposure ◆ *Eye Opening* ◆ Fabulous ◆ *Fair* ◆ Fantastic ◆ *Fascinati*

Fruitful ◆ Frustrating ◆ *Fulfilling* ◆ Fun ◆ *Good* ◆ Gratifying ◆ *Grea*

Horrible ◆ *Humorous* ◆ Important ◆ *Impressive* ◆ Incredible ◆ *Ind*

Insincere ◆ Inspirational ◆ *Inspiring* ◆ Intellectual ◆ *Intense* ◆ Inter

Invigorating ◆ *Involved* ◆ Knowledge ◆ *Learning* ◆ Learning-Exp

Mandatory ◆ Meaningful ◆ *Meaningless* ◆ Mediocre ◆ *Memorable* ◆

Motivating ◆ Motivational ◆ *Multidimensional* ◆ Multi-Faceted ◆

Opportunistic ◆ *Opportunity* ◆ Outstanding ◆ *Overview* ◆ Overwhelm

Powerful ◆ *Practical* ◆ Priceless ◆ *Productive* ◆ Professional ◆ *Realist*

Required ◆ *Research* ◆ Resourceful ◆ *Response* ◆ Resume-Builder

Satisfying ◆ Scam ◆ *Scientific* ◆ Semi-Rewarding ◆ *Sensational* ◆ S

Stimulating ◆ *Stressful* ◆ Structured ◆ *Sub-Par* ◆ Successful ◆ *Suffi*

Terrifying ◆ Thrilling ◆ *Time-Consuming* ◆ Tiring ◆ *Tolerable* ◆ Trans

Unforgettable ◆ *Unfulfilling* ◆ Uninteresting ◆ *Unique* ◆ Unpaid ◆ *Unp*

Useful ◆ Useless ◆ *Valuable* ◆ Varied ◆ *Versatile* ◆ Wake-Up-Call ◆

Aesthetic ◆ *Affirming* ◆ Amazing ◆ *Ambitious* ◆ Amusing ◆ *Arousing*

Boring ◆ Breathtaking ◆ *Busy* ◆ Careerism ◆ *Challenging* ◆ Changing

l ◆ *Creative* ◆ Crucial ◆ *Decent* ◆ Decision-Changing ◆ *Delightful*

l ◆ Disorganized ◆ *Dissatisfied* ◆ Diverse ◆ *Draining* ◆ Dull ◆ *Dynamic*

npowering ◆ *Encouraging* ◆ Energizing ◆ *Engaging* ◆ Enjoyable

Exceptional ◆ Exhausting ◆ *Exhilarating* ◆ Experience ◆ *Exploratory*

aced ◆ *Fine* ◆ Flattering ◆ *Flexible* ◆ Focusing ◆ *Fresh* ◆ Friendly

◆ *Grueling* ◆ Happy ◆ *Hard* ◆ Hectic ◆ *Hell* ◆ Helpful ◆ *Horrendous*

◆ Influential ◆ *Informal* ◆ Informational ◆ *Innovative* ◆ Insightful

terdisciplinary ◆ Interested ◆ *International* ◆ Intriguing ◆ *Invaluable*

Lesson ◆ Life Changing ◆ *Life-Altering* ◆ Long ◆ *Lousy* ◆ Magical

entorship ◆ Misleading ◆ *Mixed* ◆ Mixture ◆ *Moderate* ◆ Monotonous

◆ Networking ◆ *New* ◆ Nice ◆ *Nightmare* ◆ Observational ◆ *Okay*

l ◆ Paperwork ◆ *Perfect* ◆ Phenomenal ◆ *Pointless* ◆ Poor ◆ *Positive*

ty ◆ *Reality Check* ◆ Relationships ◆ *Relaxed* ◆ Relevant ◆ *Remarkable*

ng ◆ Rewarding ◆ *Rollercoaster* ◆ Routine ◆ *Sales* ◆ Satisfactory

low ◆ Spectacular ◆ *Spine-Tingling* ◆ Spontaneous ◆ *Stepping Stone*

itable ◆ *Superb* ◆ Surprising ◆ *Sweet* ◆ Tedious ◆ *Terrible* ◆ Terrific

◆ *Tremendous* ◆ Trying ◆ *Tumultuous* ◆ Unbelievable ◆ *Unexpected*

◆ Unproductive ◆ *Unrelated* ◆ Unsatisfactory ◆ *Unstructured* ◆ Uplifting

aste ◆ *Well- Rounded* ◆ Wonderful ◆ *Work* ◆ Worthless ◆ *Worthwhile*

OFF-BOARDING

Unlike full-time, part-time, or temporary employees, the off-boarding process in an internship program is something to be celebrated. With an internship program, there is a definitive end to the time the student will be spending with your organization (at least as an intern.) Just over 60% of interns reported that the organization provided them with an appropriate farewell at the conclusion of the program.

Showing Appreciation

Off-boarding correctly is very important. It is an organization's last opportunity to show appreciation to the students for the work that they have done. While off-boarding won't make or break the ambassadorship of a student, it could certainly bolster the organization in the student's mind as a great place to work. The process is simple, and does not have to be expensive. Several students reported that the organization took them out to lunch, or gave them company products with a thank you note. Whatever you choose to do, be sure to show appreciation!

Gain Valuable Feedback

The other critical component to the off-boarding process is your opportunity to gain valuable feedback from the student as to what they thought the strengths and weaknesses of your program were. This "exit information" will allow you to identify which pieces of your program are successful and which parts need improvement. You will be able to use quantitative and qualitative information from these exit interviews and surveys when marketing the internship program to prospective candidates.

Extending Job Offers

If your internship program is geared towards students that will be graduating soon, you may want to consider offering a full-time position as the program wraps up. Depending on the major of the student, there are traditional times of the year when official offers are made. For example, financial positions tend to be offered during the fall semester where marketing and HR offers are traditionally made in the spring. It is best to speak with a professional association within your industry to determine what time of year is best to extend the official offer. However, there is nothing precluding you from informing an intern at the conclusion of the program that you will be extending them an offer at some point. Students place great value in receiving this opportunity, and you should provide it before another organization has the chance to.

WHAT IF MY ORGANIZATION EXTENDS A FULL-TIME OFFER AND IT IS REJECTED?

Is our program a failure?

Absolutely not. This is an expectation that your organization must have from the outset of your program. Not every student who participates in your program will accept a full-time job offer. This should not discourage you from continuing your program. There are many benefits to hosting an internship program, even when students do not accept full-time positions.

Keep these important points in mind:

- Your organization is creating an extensive network of colleagues and students. Assuming that your interns have a positive experience and become ambassadors to your organization, they will share these experiences on-campus and your organization will achieve tremendous positive public relations and improve your campus recruiting brand.

- Would you rather have a well-informed candidate decline an offer because they know your organization is not a good fit for them, or an ill-informed candidate who accepts a job offer only to quit six months down the road?

- The program has provided an excellent opportunity for young managers and executives to gain a deep understanding of how to manage people, millennials in particular.

- Your organization has been able to complete work at a fraction of the cost of a full-time employee.

- The intern provided a fresh perspective and brought the most cutting-edge education and technology to the table.

- The intern could very well return to work for your organization at some point.

COMPENSATION AND BENEFITS

One of the most stressed over pieces of an internship program that organizations worry about is the topic of compensation. You have asked yourself repeatedly, "Should we pay interns? If we do, how much should we pay them? Maybe they can just get college credit?" And if you are like the majority of your peers, just when you think you have the answer someone says something that challenges your decision and makes you uncertain that you made the right one. If you are anxious about compensation when you are planning your internship program, you should be. Compensating interns, as with considering compensation for full-time employees, is a very sensitive and real issue.

> *"TOO MANY internships are unrealistic. They are positions that are not well-defined, and often students are not paid for them. It is unrealistic to think that a student can manage classes and an internship, and still try to work a job to get by. I think many programs forget that students need to make money, too. It's very important to think about."*
>
> *"I THINK that getting paid is important. It is difficult for poor students to gain access to opportunities such as an internship when they also have to work a paying job."*
>
> *"IT WAS difficult to complete an internship that consumed so much of my time and not being paid for it. It's hard to work 50 hours a week and at the end of the week not have a pay check to take home. Having to commute to the internship each day cost me money in gas and it's difficult when the money to pay for that gas is not returned. The internship put me at a financial loss."*
>
> *"I DIDN'T like how little I was paid for the amount of work I did. I knew that people who did less work than me were making more money because they were hired through a temp agency."*
>
> *"IF THE pay is competitive and actually resembles the cost of living or some other practical measure, then interns will not have to sacrifice their private lives in pursuit of professional ones."*

All Internship Compensation Should Be Created Equal

If your organization is intent on hiring more than one intern in a given discipline, be sure to pay the interns the same and offer them the same benefits. If interns are being hired in different areas of the organization, it is not necessary to pay the same wages. Some internship positions traditionally earn considerably more (sometimes double) than other positions.

College Credit Is Not Compensation

An easy way to upset a university is to claim that you are providing college credit to a student as their compensation. There needs to be an understanding that your organization does not provide college credit, the university does. Further, different universities have different requirements regarding what the student needs to do in order to earn academic credit. The student may be required to take a class or write essays. Furthermore, many universities require that students pay in order to receive credit as the result of an internship experience.

Are Organizations Creating a Disparate Impact?

Disparate impact is a legal theory used for proving unlawful employment discrimination. Time and time again, we hear stories of students working several jobs just to be able to stay in college. Some students are in such a financial pinch that they simply cannot afford to take part in an unpaid internship program. Even if the internship program is the absolute best program on earth, the bottom line here is that by making that program unpaid, an organization is excluding a large group of highly qualified candidates.

To ensure that your internship program is non-discriminatory, that the candidate pool is as large as possible, and to show universities and students that you value the contributions of interns and that your organization takes the program seriously, paying your interns should be a very important consideration.

Compensation Data

The average intern compensation is $11.96 across all academic majors, industries, and positions. Please refer to **Appendix D** for a breakdown and specific details.

Legal Implications

There is a discussion of the legal impact of unpaid internships later in this publication.

Benefits

Having a great benefits package is what could separate your internship program from the rest. Benefits, in the case of internships, are slightly different than the type of benefits that an employer might consider for full-time or part-time employees. While there are several "standard" benefits that should be employed for interns (for example, vacation days), there are also benefits that could most likely be ignored when dealing with an internship program (for example, health insurance.)

When dealing with benefits in an internship program, we are referring to any compensation or benefit for the intern, not including any compensation arising from their regular wage (if any.) This includes typical benefits as well as intern-only "perks."

Benefits are one of the main material ways in which an organization can show appreciation for work done. Interns, sometimes the most overworked employees in an organization, should certainly be considered.

As the data from the survey is self explanatory, we will not go into detail here about each of the items listed on the next two pages.

Internship Work Counts Towards Time Worked if Job Offer Is Extended

This is a fantastic way to reward interns for their work. It is also a great way to entice an intern to accept an offer of full-time employment after graduation. Depending upon how your organization operates, you may have rigid policies regarding promotions based on the length of time an employee works. The work an intern completes could be quite substantial when applied to this time. For example, if a summer intern working full-time were allowed to have "intern time" counted, it could account for almost 4,000 hours of completed employment.

Brown Bag Lunches

The idea of "brown bag lunches" has been creeping up in internship programs of all sizes, industries, and job functions. The main purpose of the brown bag lunch is to give interns the opportunity to meet different director-level and higher-up professionals within the organization. In many organizations, the brown bag lunches are lead by "chief" level personnel. From the survey, 98% of students believed that the organization should provide a chance for them to explore other career opportunities outside of the department where they are assigned during the internship. 77% of interns reported that they were actually given this chance, a 21% gap.

> *"THE COMPANY I worked for was both small and on the cutting edge of their industry. It was great to have direct access to the people who were making important decisions and leading the pack in the field."*

SURVEY DISCUSSION

Table G shows the benefits available to interns, as reported by organizations.

Rank	Benefits to Interns: Reported by Organizations	# of Organizations	% of Organizations
1	Free/subsidized parking	74	41%
2	Social events for interns to meet one another	37	21%
3	Discounted organization merchandise or services	21	12%
4	Internship work counts towards time worked if job offer is extended	21	12%
5	Transportation stipend	16	9%
6	Free organization merchandise or services	14	8%
7	Fitness center membership	14	8%
8	Meal allowance	14	7%
9	Vacation pay	12	7%
10	Sporting event tickets	11	6%
11	Partial housing assistance	7	4%
12	Theater tickets	6	3%
13	Partial relocation assistance	4	2%
14	Complete housing assistance	3	2%
15	Health insurance	3	2%
16	Commission on sales (if applicable)	3	2%
17	Uniform stipend	2	1%
18	Full benefits (same as full time employees)	2	1%
19	Tuition reimbursement	1	1%

Table H shows the benefits available to interns, as reported by interns.

Rank	Benefits to Interns: Reported by Interns	# of Interns	% of Interns
	Table H - Benefits Available to Interns - Reported by Interns		
1	Free/subsidized parking	584	37%
2	Social events for interns to meet one another	370	23%
3	Free organization merchandise or services	233	15%
4	Transportation stipend	214	13%
5	Discounted organization merchandise or services	187	12%
6	Meal allowance	184	12%
7	Fitness center membership	149	9%
8	Sporting event tickets	149	9%
9	Internship work counts towards time worked if job offer is extended	88	6%
10	Theater tickets	85	5%
11	Complete housing assistance	83	5%
12	Vacation pay	79	5%
13	Uniform stipend	59	4%
14	Full benefits (same as full time employees)	53	3%
15	Health insurance	42	3%
16	Partial housing assistance	35	2%
17	Commission on sales (if applicable)	33	2%
18	Complete relocation assistance	26	2%
19	Tuition reimbursement	23	1%
20	Partial relocation assistance	17	1%

Brown bag lunches are an inexpensive way to give interns a glimpse into other job functions within your organization. Depending on cost constraints, students can be asked to bring their own lunch, or the organization can provide lunch. Brown bag lunches usually last for one hour. The presenter will typically speak about how they became involved in that particular field of work, how they rose to the top, and offer advice for the interns. Be sure to provide ample time for interns to ask questions. Brown bag lunches are almost always informal events.

> *"MY FAVORITE part of the internship was the weekly meetings with all of the interns to learn about the different aspects of the business."*

Organizational Gifts

Almost every single intern who was employed by an organization that provides a service or sold a product reported receiving some sort of gift of that organization's service or product. For example, interns reported receiving free shoes from a shoe manufacturer, tickets to a concert from a radio station, branded hats and jackets from a television station, and food from a restaurant business. This is yet another inexpensive way to show interns appreciation.

Off-site Organization Functions

When an organization conducts an off-site function, the interns should be included. Whether it is the summer barbecue or the annual meeting, interns appreciate being invited to these events. It provides them with a sense of belonging, and it gives them a great feeling of community. It will also give them the chance to network with additional personnel and to learn more about the organization.

Tour of Organization or Industry-Related Sites and Buildings

Some interns reported being given access to special "behind the scenes" tours of organizations or industry-related sites. Interns working in theater were given tours of the backstage area; interns working in event management were given the chance to go backstage at concerts; and interns working in the finance area report being given tours of high-security areas in the New York Stock Exchange. These types of tours provide an intern with an even more in-depth preview of what it might be like to work in that particular industry.

Opportunity to Attend Company Trainings

Organizations tend to host internal training and seminars for their employees not only for specific job-related skills, but also in "hot topics" such as mediation skills or time management. Allowing interns to attend these programs is a significant benefit that provides for excellent experiential education opportunities.

Lunches and Birthday Cake

An easy and inexpensive way for an organization to show that they care is to provide lunches and birthday cake for interns. As simple as this may sound, it was one of the most noted benefits when interns were asked open-ended questions relating to benefits they received. In particular, there appeared to be a high level of intern satisfaction when their supervisor took them out to (and paid for) lunch, or brought them coffee in the morning. When the intern applies to work for the organization, they will provide their birth date. A special note should be made in the supervisor's calendar if the birthday falls during the internship time frame. Several interns reported that they were given birthday cake, birthday cards, balloons, a surprise party within their department, and small gifts such as a gift basket or movie tickets.

Idea Presentation

As discussed earlier, one of the main reasons for hosting an internship program is to allow students with a fresh prospective and the most up-to-date education to have an impact within an organization. One method to ensure that interns are contributing their innovative ideas is to provide them with a forum to present those ideas. This presentation technique can take on many forms. It can be in a report form that is submitted to the director of the department, or the vice president. Several interns reported that their host organizations held an "internship idea fair." In this setting, similar to a grade school science fair, interns would create poster boards of their ideas for employees of the organization to view and inquire about.

The idea can also be large scale. One intern noted that his host organization provided for a competition. Interns presented various ideas to top-level officials. If even a small part of the idea was ultimately implemented, the intern received special recognition and some sort of prize. The opportunity to envision an idea for an organization, and then have that idea exhibited to employees of the organization is very exciting for interns.

Preferential Interview

Offering interns the chance for preferential interview times is perceived to be a great benefit. If an organization either has high turnover, or is growing quickly, allowing current (or past) interns to have a preference in the interview process is an easy benefit to implement with a relatively large impact to interns. From an organization's perspective, this benefit should make sense. After all, the intern would have been "interviewing" over the course of many weeks. Most organizations give internal employees the opportunity to fill positions before the organization looks externally. Interns should be treated the same in this practice.

Skill Development Sessions

Skills workshops can be of great value to an intern. In particular, students are almost always interested in learning ways to better apply their leadership, presentation, and communication skills. Providing a workshop for interns geared toward the improvement of these skills (or several others) can help an intern become more confident, and more effective in the work they complete for their host organization. These programs should be conducted towards the beginning of the internship experience so that the organization can maximize their benefit. It is not necessary to bring in a special consultant or trainer to carry out the programming. Remember that interns are impressionable students, eager to learn more about the world of work. Having someone within your organization manage the workshops would certainly be sufficient.

Resume Workshops

While most colleges and universities have career development departments that will critique a student's resume, the opportunity to have their resume critiqued by a professional in the industry is a huge benefit. A resume workshop could be conducted by someone in the HR department or by several different individuals on a rotating basis. If individuals are hired in an organization by department managers, having a rotation where the resume is critiqued by managers from different departments will provide the intern with constructive criticism from several different angles.

Industry Exams and Credentials

Several interns reported that their organizations assisted them in obtaining certain industry certifications and licensure. For example, if the intern works in the Human Resources department, the department may wish to assist the intern obtaining their PHR credentials by reimbursing the student for a prep class or for the exam fee. Several students working in the financial sector reported that their employers helped them to pay for their Series 7 examination.

ALCOHOL AND INTERNS

> *"MY INTERNSHIP rocked because I loved my boss and colleagues. I got to attend meetings and represent [the company], I got to do research and create websites, write reports, go out to bars with the entire team, and make presentations."*

The quote above represents a recurring theme found in the research data. Many interns reported that they were provided alcohol by their host sites. Sometimes the beverages were provided during meals, and other times at organization-wide events. Generally speaking, interns appreciate the gesture and will take an employer up on their offer. The main reason for this stems from the obvious social context of acceptance into a group. In many cases, interns feel that sharing a drink with the boss means they have earned their keep.

But there is more than just providing the alcohol that needs to be considered. The National Association of Colleges and Employers, the largest nationwide association for bringing together the two entities, issued a "principle document" in 1998 regarding this very issue. The bottom line is this: employers are discouraged from furnishing alcohol to interns, and for good reason.

First there is the obvious legal implication – how closely will your organization monitor the age of your interns? You can't ask it during an interview, so how likely is it that you will go back and review internal documents to figure out their age based on their birthday? Providing alcohol to minors is a serious crime, and it will open your organization up to an incredible amount of criminal and civil liability.

Then there are the ethical arguments. Take into consideration the student who chooses not to drink alcohol in general, but, when offered by their employer, feels obligated to do so to fit in. What if that individual is unfamiliar with their "alcohol tolerance?" They could embarrass themselves, or worse.

There also needs to be consideration of the university where the student attends. Many colleges have strictly "alcohol free" campuses. By offering alcohol to interns in violation of these policies, you could seriously jeopardize the relationships that your organization has with the college moving forward.

The principle document was adopted by the ethics committee of NACE. As an employer who is either a member of NACE, or is thinking of joining (more information in Appendix E), you may end up adopting a position that you comply with the NACE "Principles of Professional Conduct." (You should – it means a lot to universities.) If your organization does take that position, you should strongly consider not serving alcohol to interns.

Additional Benefit Ideas:

- Cruises
- Theater tickets
- Company beach bags
- Company back packs
- Company key chains
- Bowling trips
- Fleece shirts
- T-shirts / Polo shirts
- Water bottles
- Deck of cards
- Pens and pencils
- Mugs
- Luggage tags
- Digital cameras
- Gift cards to retailers and restaurants
- Gift bags
- Comedy show tickets
- Discount movie tickets
- Massages
- Intern raffles

THE MANAGER'S GUIDE TO COACHING AND DELIVERING FEEDBACK TO THE COLLEGE INTERN

Joseph R. Weintraub, Ph.D. and James Hunt, DBA
Division of Management, Babson College

Introduction

The internship experience provides students with the opportunity to gain experience in the "real world" while, hopefully, adding value to the sponsoring organization and individual. Sponsors can play a significant role in shaping the interns' personal and professional development. A key ingredient in providing this learning opportunity is the sponsor's willingness and ability to deliver quality coaching and feedback to student interns. We recognize that finding time to coach and deliver feedback is an issue in most organizations. Since interns will generally spend a limited time in most sponsoring organizations, such time constraints can represent a significant challenge. However, since most companies also want to benefit from the internship experience, we would argue that the business case for providing coaching and feedback to interns is quite compelling.

While the principles of coaching and delivering feedback to college interns are based on the same principles used in other organizational settings, it is important to understand that college interns are different than other employees. Interns are typically students who may or may not end up working in their sponsoring organization after they complete their education. Because many of these students are relatively young and inexperienced with the world of work, the host organizations and the people who supervise and work with these students have the opportunity to provide a meaningful developmental experience for their interns. In fact, early boss-intern experiences are often among the most impactful in shaping how students will see future work experiences including the students' attitudes about work and even their eventual leadership approach.

Coaching

The use of coaching can make a positive difference in the internship experience for the intern, supervisor and company. While there are many approaches to coaching, we will discuss our developmental model that we strongly recommend when dealing with college interns. Much of what will be presented is based on our earlier published work and has been adapted here for use with college interns (see *The Coaching Manager: Developing Top Talent in Business* by James Hunt and Joseph Weintraub (Sage Publications, 2002) and *The Coaching Organization: A Strategy for Developing Leaders*, by James Hunt and

Joseph Weintraub (Sage Publications, 2007)). The modification of our original "Coaching Manager" model is referred to in this chapter as *The Weintraub-Hunt Model for Coaching College Interns* which integrates our approach to organizational coaching with the current research efforts of Richard Bottner (2007) who examined college internship experiences.

The Weintraub-Hunt Model for Coaching College Interns: A Developmental Approach

The Weintraub-Hunt Model for Coaching College Interns offers an opportunity for companies and the people who manage college interns to increase the growth and learning of the interns within their respective organizations. The utility of our developmental approach has been demonstrated consistently in our consulting work and through our 10 years of research with over 7,500 students and coaches at Babson College in Wellesley, Massachusetts in the Coaching for Leadership and Teamwork Program (www.babson.edu/coach).

The developmental approach used in our model is learner-focused—coaching is targeted at what the learner hopes to learn. The approach is oriented toward learning and change rather than on compliance. The model also helps the intern/learner to capitalize on existing strengths as much or more than on overcoming weaknesses.

The table below outlines the major components of the model.

Weintraub-Hunt Model for Coaching College Interns: A Developmental Approach
Selecting Coachable Interns
Defining Successful Performance
Creating a Coaching-Friendly Context
Stopping the Action: Creating Coaching Moments
The Coaching Dialogue: Asking Good Questions
Providing Balanced Feedback
Creating a Developmental Plan
Following-Up

Based on James Hunt and Joseph Weintraub, *The Coaching Manager: Developing Top Talent in Business*, Sage Publications, 2002

Selecting Coachable Interns

In order for coaching to be an effective process in internship programs, the students who are selected for internships must be carefully screened and chosen for their willingness to learn and to be coached. Southwest Airlines is a good example of an organization that makes a strong effort to select people with the right "attitude" to do the job. With interns, it is important for them to understand that they will receive coaching and that they will be active participants in what is hopefully a positive learning experience.

Defining Successful Performance

If you have the right talent, the intern's supervisor needs to explain what success would look like for the intern and the organization. Defining success can be done by clearly explaining the major roles and responsibilities and/or describing the results that would constitute success, during the internship as well as at the internship's conclusion.

This step is often missed, leaving the intern and the organization confused and disappointed. It becomes very difficult to provide appropriate coaching if there isn't a clear set of expectations about the criteria for success. Not understanding the culture is one of the major reasons people at all levels fail in organizations—so, it is important to spend the time early on to define the job and to discuss how things actually work in the company's corporate culture.

Creating a Coaching-Friendly Context

Interns can often feel lost and disconnected if they are not properly welcomed to the organization. It starts on Day 1 by appropriately introducing the interns to the people they will be working with.

Letting interns know that they don't have to have all the answers and that it is okay to ask for help are simple but key concepts in creating a positive work environment. The supervisor's willingness to help and develop the intern also plays a big role in overall success.

Stopping the Action: Creating Coaching Moments

At different intervals (once a week or once every two weeks) it is important to check in with the intern to discuss the internship experience. These check-ins send a powerful message to the intern about the importance of the internship experience. There are also unscheduled coaching moments that occur when you may have observed a significant event. For example, having a chance to talk with the intern soon after the completion of a significant customer interaction is a great opportunity to have the intern reflect and learn from the experience.

The Coaching Dialogue: Asking Good Questions

Of all the strategies for working with interns, sitting down with the intern and asking questions about their experience are essential behaviors if student learning is a key goal of the internship experience. The developmental coaching model has, at its core, the use of effective questioning as a fundamental process. It is highly recommended that interns receive frequent coaching and that the supervisor's coaching approach includes the use of questioning (versus lecturing). For example, after a project was completed, a supervisor might ask questions such as "How did that go?" "What was it like?" "How did it feel" "What were you trying to accomplish?" "What did you learn?" and "How do you plan to use the learning from this internship?" The use of questions in a positive tone demonstrates the supervisor's willingness to understand the intern's experience from the student perspective.

Providing Balanced Feedback

Student interns are in a learning mode. They are not necessarily, at this stage of their development, polished and knowledgeable about the job or the organization. So, it is important to balance the need to deliver good feedback with the understanding that we want to help the intern to become better. This is where the connection between coaching and feedback makes a difference. Blending a developmental coaching orientation along with good feedback often works best when dealing with interns. A more thorough look at feedback will be presented later in the chapter.

Creating a Developmental Plan

Most interns don't get a lot of time to interact with their internship supervisors. But to get the most out of the internship experience, it is highly recommended that part of the coaching process include the creation of a developmental plan during the internship itself. This plan should be developed jointly by interns and their supervisors and should focus on defining goals for the internship itself, as well as for the personal/professional goals of the intern. The conversation with the intern about the plan is essential and sends a strong message that the organization cares about its interns, both during and after the internship experience. This conversation often lasts from 30-60 minutes and with an emphasis on what the intern would like to learn.

Following-up

In spite of good intentions to develop interns, a follow-up coaching schedule to check in on progress for the intern's developmental plan is highly recommended. The follow-up should happen as part of the internship assignment itself and at the conclusion of the internship assignment. This coaching step takes time but it sends a powerful message that the organization cares about the personal development of its interns. Besides being a good thing to do for interns, the word-of-mouth "advertising" from the interns about the organization's commitment to its interns also pays huge dividends for future recruiting efforts.

PROVIDING FEEDBACK TO COLLEGE INTERNS

Good developmental coaching typically involves the use of feedback. But one distinction that is critical to remember is that feedback, by itself, is not necessarily coaching. Telling an intern that he "blew it" in delivering a presentation is feedback, but it is certainly not developmental coaching. However, feedback is one of the most important parts of the internship experience. We recognize that finding time to deliver feedback is an issue in most organizations. And since interns will generally leave the organization in a relatively short period of time, feedback is often a challenge to do well.

The Benefits of Feedback

The benefits of feedback, especially when combined with appropriate levels of coaching, can be enormous for both company and interns alike. As such, developing skill in effectively providing feedback to employees should be considered an important goal for all supervisors of interns. From prior research on the benefits of employee feedback (London, 1997), the following applications also apply to student interns:

- Feedback can help interns set appropriate goals for themselves and the internship itself. On the basis of the feedback that interns receive, they can see what they have accomplished. Those who are motivated will want to achieve even more.

- Positive feedback, when appropriate, can help interns feel that they have achieved something even when their achievement doesn't necessarily lead to a final result, such as project completion. Some projects, for example, will be completed after the intern has left to return to school.

- Motivation theory and research also show that feedback can serve to enhance motivation since interns will understand what it takes to be successful. They will know the rules of the road. The intern who can say, "Now I know how to get there" is more likely to make the attempt.

- Feedback can also help interns see what they need to learn. They have a clearer sense of their own weaknesses or learning gaps. Their ability to take charge of their own development is enhanced.

- People who are used to getting feedback tend to seek it out. Effective provision of feedback by a manager is one of the most important tactics for creating a coaching-friendly context that should be the goal of every intern's manager.

Key Elements in Delivering Feedback

Feedback represents a form of communication, or a message. What should the message include? Feedback content usually includes the following:

- A description of the situation in which you observed the intern;
- A description of the behavior of, or actions taken by, the intern you observed;
- Finally, a description of the impact of the behavior or actions of the intern on others or on a relevant business outcome. "Here is what I saw, and here is what I think was the impact of what I saw" is the basic structure of a feedback message.

Note what is included and not included in the message. What is included is factual information, to the highest degree possible. What is not included is an interpretation.

You may have to climb the ladder of inference a bit when describing what you "think" is the impact of a particular action or behavior; but oftentimes, you'll know. You'll know because you can describe the impact of the intern's behavior on you. "I don't know what others might have thought about your approach to this, but I liked it. It really addressed my concerns." If you describe the impact from your vantage point, you're making very few inferences. After all, an individual's manager is a key stakeholder in the actions of that individual. The impact on you as manager of the intern does count, and the impact you experience from the actions of an intern may be similar to the impact experienced by others. You can therefore state, "This was the impact on me" with real authority.

On the basis of our own research and review of the literature on personal learning, we strongly encourage you to always consider the importance of the intern's goals while delivering feedback. If you focus on what the intern is trying to accomplish or has told you he or she wants to learn, you have been given greater license by the intern to be clear and direct.

Setting the Stage for Feedback

We encourage you to always set the stage in such a way that the self-esteem of the intern will be minimally threatened. Deliver feedback in a way that is sensitive to the intern's needs. The old rule "Praise in public, criticize in private" should serve as your guide.

Setting the stage also involves a consideration of timing. Feedback, particularly if it is based on data collected from others, could be a source of anxiety for the intern. Substantial feedback takes time to absorb. If you are going to engage in a major feedback conversation, make sure you and the intern have sufficient time to thoroughly discuss the issues raised by the feedback.

Feedback that is given right after an action and the individual's reflection on that action is more likely to result in learning. The events are fresh in everyone's mind. Feedback that is timely is thus important as well. It may be necessary for you to take a few minutes to figure out what you want to say, but don't delay too long.

The feedback you provide should be specific and focused on the task, action, or behavior. By specific, we mean descriptive. It is important to gather data that accurately reflect the intern's performance. Feedback involves delivering that data in a way that is helpful.

For the receiver of feedback to be able to make use of the data provided by their supervisor, the information must be presented clearly and simply. The language and style of the feedback are important—avoid nondescriptive or technical terms unless you are sure that the receiver of the feedback can work with those terms and can understand what they actually mean.

The best feedback is also usually quite direct. Directness usually requires the use of "I" statements. "This is what I saw." Some of us have experienced, and probably all of us have heard about, feedback statements that begin, "We don't think ..." The reality is that, unless the intern knows who you are talking about when you use the word "we," such a feedback statement may have very little credibility. "We" statements can also make the intern feel "ganged-up on" or attacked. If the supervisor has to provide feedback on behalf of several individuals, it is much more effective to be specific about who said what. We also feel strongly that feedback to interns and to all employees should always be intended to maintain or enhance the individual's self-esteem. So, the way we deliver feedback is critical to the intern's ability to learn and reflect.

Avoid unfounded inferences; such interpretations are likely to generate defensiveness—and worse yet, are likely to be wrong. Our favorite example of inference disguised as feedback is "You have a bad attitude." Such a statement is actually devoid of data and represents a pure interpretation. A descriptive statement that would support such an interpretation might be something like "You told the last three customers who walked in the door that you hated working here and that you can't wait to go back to school." Note that such a descriptive statement is in some ways even more hard-hitting than the interpretation. Data almost always carry more weight than the inappropriate use of inference.

Finally, ask the intern what he or she can or will do with the feedback. Ideally, feedback leads to additional reflection, and then action. Having delivered the feedback, or after delivering each point of the feedback, the intern's supervisor should stop, make sure that he or she was understood, and ask for the intern's thoughts about how the feedback can help. Remember that the coaching process in this feedback process begins with a coaching dialogue. It is important to keep the dialogue going by providing plenty of opportunity for the employee to reflect on the feedback you have provided. A little silence during these periods is okay. It is far better to offer some feedback, ask for the intern's reactions, and then wait, rather than hurry on to the next point. Indeed, if the feedback has any real substance to it, it is natural for the intern to need a few minutes to digest what has been said. Make sure you, the supervisor, don't do all the talking!

After the feedback is given, the intern may move ahead with future reflection and action. If the feedback is particularly negative or problematic, however, it may be wise to schedule another meeting to follow up soon after the meeting at which the feedback was given. Even under the best of circumstances, critical feedback can be difficult for some interns to manage, so don't try to overdo the giving of feedback. Keep your list short, except in the case of delivering positive feedback where, in most cases, interns will not be as uncomfortable in receiving good news! Follow-up meetings show concern for the intern and symbolize the supervisor's commitment to the intern's ongoing learning.

The Lack of Feedback

We know from our consulting work in organizations that most people do not receive feedback or, if they do, they don't receive feedback that is perceived as helpful. It is critical, therefore, that interns receive feedback. The old adage that "some feedback, even negative, is better than no feedback at all" is generally true. It is also true that missing or incomplete spoken feedback does not mean that the intern gets no feedback at all. Inaction on the part of the manager is also feedback. The intern will often fill in the gaps. The intern will particularly wonder, "Did I do a good job?" and/or "Does the manager think I can really handle this?" Ultimately, like it or not, the intern will be thinking about questions such as "Does she like me?" "Am I doing a good job?" "Does anyone here care about me?" and "Is this a good manager to be working for?"

According to most research on learning, feedback offered without the support of coaching will often not be all that helpful to the student intern. As stated earlier, feedback should be delivered to the intern in a "helpful" way. The lesson here is to look for opportunities to deliver feedback to an intern that is constructive and helpful without feeling that you have to give a daily report card—after all, the interns wanted a departure from grading. What you can give, however, is the gift of your coaching and feedback to our future employees and leaders.

Joseph R. Weintraub

B.S., University of Pittsburgh; M.A. and Ph.D. in Industrial-Organizational Psychology, Bowling Green State University

Dr. Weintraub is a Professor of Management and Organizational Behavior at Babson College. He serves as faculty director in leadership programs for Babson Executive Education as well as being the founder and Co-Director of the Coaching for Leadership and Teamwork Program at Babson. He also has supervised Undergraduate and MBA students for over 15 years in Babson's field study programs. In addition to his work at Babson, he is the president of Organizational Dimensions, a management consulting and leadership development firm in Wellesley, Massachusetts. Dr. Weintraub is the coauthor of The Coaching Manager: Developing Top Talent in Business (Sage, 2002) and The Coaching Organization: A Strategy for Developing Leaders (Sage, 2007).

James M. Hunt

Associate Professor of Management
B. Sc., Massachusetts Institute of Technology; M.S.W., Simmons College; D.B.A., Boston University

Dr. Hunt is Associate Professor of Management and Chair of the Management Division at Babson College in Wellesley, Massachusetts, where he teaches management, strategic human resource management and leadership at the graduate and executive education levels. He is currently the Charles Barton Term Chair Holder. Dr. Hunt is a faculty member of the Leadership and Influence Program at the Babson College School of Executive Education and is Faculty Co-Director of the Coaching for Leadership and Teamwork Program at Babson. He is co-author of two recent books, The Coaching Manager: Developing Top Talent in Business, and The Coaching Organization: A Strategy for Leadership Development available from Sage Publications.

References

- Bottner, Richard. Northeast Internship Study, Acton, MA: Intern Bridge 2007.
- Hunt, James and Weintraub, Joseph. *The Coaching Manager: Developing Top Talent in Business*, Thousand Oaks, CA: Sage Publications, 2002.
- Hunt, James and Weintraub, Joseph. *The Coaching Organization: A Strategy for Developing Leaders*, Thousand Oaks, CA: Sage Publications, 2007.
- London, M. Job Feedback. Mahwah, NJ: Lawrence Erlbaum, 1997.

PROGRAM ASSESSMENT

Effimia Parpos
Associate Director, Alumni Association, Suffolk University
Former Associate Director, Career Education, Babson College

What is Assessment?

Simply stated, assessment is the process of measuring individual or program outcomes. Assessment can be conducted using a systematic approach in which both quantitative and qualitative data is collected, or by using a less formal method. While the former is more likely to yield valid results, data collected from the latter method also has merit. In fact, depending upon the culture of an organization, the philosophical views of a particular manager/supervisor (referred to as manager throughout the remainder of this chapter), or the reason(s) for conducting assessment, one of the aforementioned processes for collecting the data may be perceived as having more value add.

The bottom line is that most organizations and colleges/universities, as well as managers and career service professionals (and faculty, when appropriate), use assessment data to guide decision-making in partnerships, strategic business initiatives, and staffing.

Why is Assessment Important?

In recent years, there has been an increased focus on assessment. In addition to evaluating the performance of team members, managers have been instructed to provide evidence of program success that goes beyond anecdotal stories and to demonstrate the value-add of programs in order to secure additional financial resources. This directive to measure outcomes on individual and programmatic levels is not limited to Fortune 500 companies, but is also strongly encouraged and even required at small, mid-size, and large organizations that recruit and hire interns and maintain internship programs.

Managers assess interns and internship programs for a wide variety of reasons:

- To provide evidence regarding whether or not a student benefited from an internship.
- To demonstrate the degree to which a student learned or gained new skills.
- To guide the student in identifying areas for improvement.
- To provide data regarding the overall program.
- To demonstrate value add.
- To offer suggestions for program improvement.

There is great variability regarding the degree to which managers conduct and ultimately utilize data collected from the various assessment tools. Managers who seek to recruit the best talent for their organizations or strive to strengthen the quality of their internship programs will likely leverage assessment data to inform hiring decisions, guide recruiting strategies, and make modifications to their program, be it the position description, orientation program, or strategic integration within the organizational culture.

Data from the Intern Bridge research reinforces the notion that managers not only conduct but also value assessment. More than fifty percent (54%) of managers surveyed in the study reported that their organization actively solicits feedback from interns about their experiences. Student feedback reinforced this finding. Nearly fifty percent (50%) of interns reported that their organization actively solicited feedback regarding the internship experience. Noteworthy is that nearly fifty percent (45%) of managers who responded to the survey reported that their organizations strive to make changes to the program based on feedback received from interns.

Individual Assessment (a.k.a. Performance Appraisals)

Perhaps, the type of assessment that we are most familiar with is performance appraisals. Depending on the organization, the performance appraisal process, including the frequency and timeline, as well as the degree to which the process is formalized, will vary.

In general, consistently evaluating staff performance using organizational guidelines is essential for monitoring progress, supporting staff to improve performance, and meeting departmental/organizational goals. In a similar manner, providing consistent and timely feedback to interns ensures that they have an opportunity to demonstrate success or improve performance during the short duration of their internship experience.

It is interesting to note that less than thirty percent (26%) of managers who participated in the research reported that interns are evaluated often. Conversely, seventy percent (70%) of interns reported that they were provided with constructive feedback. This discrepancy may be explained, in part, by a manager's style –interns may have interpreted constructive feedback, whether formal or informal, as a type of evaluation and therefore responded with favorable comments regarding assessment.

Managers assess interns' performance and contributions to an organization in numerous ways:

- **Observation:** Managers observe how interns carry out responsibilities and the ways in which they collaborate with members of the organization. These observations provide valuable feedback about a wide variety of skills valued by the organization, including teamwork and project management.

- **Consultation:** Because managers cannot be in all places at all times, they solicit feedback from their colleagues in all levels of the organization to provide input regarding interns' performance on tasks and accomplishments. Depending upon the intern's specific role, the manager may also consult with external constituents to gain a deeper understanding of the intern's impact.

- **Skills Training:** In addition to a general orientation to an organization, most likely an intern will participate in a training program at the outset of an internship. Typically, training programs provide an opportunity to learn new skills (e.g. analysis using particular statistical software, web site development.) Interns' ability to demonstrate skills following the training is another measure of assessment which a manager may document.

While collecting this data is valuable, more important is sharing the feedback with the intern(s). The particulars of the performance appraisal process will vary depending upon the organization, and perhaps even the manager's style. Nevertheless, it is critical for a manager to provide timely feedback regardless of whether the process is a formal mid-internship performance review or in the context of an informal discussion. Best practices for assessing interns' performance include the following:

- Setting clear expectations at the outset of the internship regarding desired outcomes.
- Establishing the parameters for providing formal feedback.
- Articulating the specific timeline for delivering feedback.
- Providing informal feedback throughout the duration of the internship experience.
- Delivering the feedback according to the pre-determined parameters.

In addition to the performance appraisal process mandated by organizations, colleges often conduct individual assessments. More specifically, colleges administer surveys to interns and to employers to solicit interns' observations of skills improvement and to gather employers' input regarding interns' performance. When colleges administer similarly structured surveys to interns and employers – often referred to as "companion surveys" – the data collected provides comparative quantitative assessment. At some colleges/universities, this information is utilized to determine letter grades or to award credit for an internship course. Depending upon the particular questions posed, the survey tool may also provide insights into program assessment.

Program Assessment

While data regarding the performance of interns and their individual contributions is important, particularly for informing hiring decisions, collecting data regarding the internship program overall is equally important. Program assessment is essential for several reasons. More specifically, program assessment:

- Assists managers to identify best practices in internship programs.
- Guides managers to identify areas for program improvement.
- Aides career services professionals to identify employers that offer quality internship programs.

A variety of tools, including surveys and focus groups, are utilized to measure program satisfaction and effectiveness. Surveys, frequently conducted online (e.g. Survey Monkey, Perseus), are a cost-effective method for collecting large quantities of data from multiple constituents – interns and employers – in a timely manner. The following are guidelines for developing the survey instrument:

- Create a short survey.
- Use a rating scale for most questions
  (it is easier to tally and score the data).
- Incorporate open-ended questions to collect qualitative data.

Focus groups are another method for collecting data. Focus groups may be structured, in which the facilitator asks participants to respond to pre-determined questions, or informal, in which the facilitator sets the stage and thereafter poses targeted questions in response to comments shared by participants.

Needs assessment is another type of evaluation. This form of assessment may be of particular use to managers and/or career service professionals when developing new internship programs. More specifically, the questions posed in a needs assessment survey focus on interns' desires or desired program outcomes.

Similar to individual assessment in which feedback is solicited from interns as well as managers, program assessment should solicit feedback from both. While assessment tools may need to be tailored for interns versus managers, it is important to provide comparative assessment. The aggregate data may inform decisions pertaining to recruiting strategies, hiring practices, intern assignments, and continued partnerships between a particular organization and a specific college/university.

Best Practices in Individual and Program Assessments

While a manager can solicit feedback from multiple sources in numerous ways, to be most effective assessment should incorporate several best practices:

- **Best Practices #1:** Create a systematic process for conducting assessment. It is not sufficient to administer satisfaction surveys, host focus groups, or conduct needs assessment; assessment needs to be an on-going and planned process. This ensures that individual contributions and program satisfaction and outcomes are documented in a timely and consistent manner in order to reward performance as well as to facilitate resource allocation or demonstrate value add to the bottom line.

- **Best Practices #2:** Establish guidelines regarding frequency and timeline for collecting data. There are several reasons why this is good practice. First, creating a data collection schedule ensures that assessment-related projects are high priority on the task list rather than completed as an afterthought. Second, compiling information collected over a period of time provides managers and organizations with historical data which may serve as a vehicle to support the hiring or promotion of an individual or an effective planning tool pertaining to program delivery and improvement. On a related note, compiling information over a period of time provides colleges/universities with insights regarding organizations which offer quality internship programs versus those that do not. Finally, the design and implementation of an assessment plan ensures the data is valid and reliable.

- **Best Practices #3:** Establish specific, measurable goals/objectives at the outset. By defining intended outcomes, interns have a clear under standing of management's expectations and their responsibilities. At the conclusion of the internship experience, using various assessment tools, they can articulate their progress on various projects and skills developed.

Furthermore, establishing goals/objectives not only provides managers with a clear vision of the internship program but also a means to effectively evaluate all components of the internship program, including structure and intern responsibilities. It is important to note that during the course of an internship, managers and interns may agree to modify goals and objectives for a wide variety of reasons.

Components of Good Internship Programs

Many organizations offer internship programs, but some programs are better than others. For an internship program to be great, it requires that you:

- Solicit support from all levels of management within your organization. Interns value the opportunity to meet and interact with key decision makers in the organization. These forums not only provide insights about operations and strategy, but also showcase the types of leadership roles which they may aspire to. Effectively engaging all levels of management in the various facets of the internship program is a primary way to demonstrate to interns that their presence and contributions are valued by the organization.

- Call on your best people to orient interns to your organization, to supervise them, and to mentor them. This will ensure that your interns have the best training and are connected to the individuals who give your organization the reputation that it has. Pairing interns with poor managers can reflect negatively on the organization and may be a contributing factor to an intern's decision to decline a job offer if one is made.

- Assign meaningful work to your intern(s). If you are using interns as a pipeline strategy for recruiting full-time hires, you will want to assign work which gives the intern an accurate picture of the work he/she would perform in their first year of employment.

And most importantly, a good internship program will provide timely feedback to an intern regarding his/her performance as well as solicit impressions regarding the overall internship experience from both interns and the managers and others involved in the internship program.

Final Thoughts...

While the purpose and scope of assessment will vary depending upon the organization or college/university, there will continue to be a demand for managers and career service professionals (and/or faculty) to assess interns and internship programs. Conducting assessment can be time-consuming and even intimidating, but the more assessment you do, the more comfortable you will become with it, and perhaps most importantly, the more likely you are to see its value.

Effimia (Effie) Parpos is Associate Director, Alumni Association at Suffolk University. She is an accomplished student services professional, with more than nine years experience in college adminis-tration, including career services and enrollment management. Effie has facilitated presentations on various career development topics at regional and national professional conferences. Prior to coming to Suffolk, Effie was Associate Director, Career Education at Babson College. During her tenure at Babson, Effie also served as Acting Director of the Undergraduate Center for Career Development. Effie's professional experience also includes Wheelock College where she served as Director of Gradu-ate Student Services as well as Director of the Center for Career Development. Effie earned a B.A. in Psychology and a Master of Social Work from Boston College.

Further Reading:

- Gordon, David, "Tracking Internship Outcomes through Comparative Quantitative Assessment." *NACE Journal*, Winter 2002, pp. 28 – 32.

- Greenberg, Robert and Harris, Marcia B., "Measuring Up: Assessment in Career Services." *NACE Journal*, December 2006, pp. 18 – 24.

- Taguchi, Sherrie Gong, "Summer Internship Programs: From Good to Great in Eight Essential Steps." *NACE Journal*, December 2006, pp. 25 – 30.4.

INCREASING DIVERSITY WITHIN INTERN POPULATIONS

Debora S. Bloom, M.A.
President, Debra Bloom Associates

Many organizations ask what they can do to diversify their workforce. One way is to establish and maintain diversity internships as part of building an organization's staffing pipeline. Internships should be positioned as part of an overall long-term talent acquisition strategy. Many organizations have done this for years and others are just beginning.

This article looks at several internship success components and also identifies some existing programs and resources. The first key to success is attracting a diverse pool of interns through a sound and broad recruitment strategy. Second is the appropriate selection and development of internship supervisors. Third is designing the experience so interns feel valued and productive while taking a major step toward their career goal. Finally, the company needs to recognize that offering diversity internships is an opportunity to publicize the organization as an inclusive, desirable workplace.

When people speak of diversity interns they usually have in mind people from particular racial or ethnic groups, which were traditionally excluded from full participation in the workforce. Now, with changing demographics and the renewed war for talent, organizations have a pressing need to attract and retain as diverse a workforce as possible. In setting up diversity internship programs, organizations may want to consider expanding their definition of diversity and their outreach efforts. Other talent pools to consider include people with disabilities or single mothers of young children.

To initiate a diversity internship program employers can research the internet to find what other organizations are doing. They can contact other employers in their own industry or locality to learn from their experience. They can check with their trade or professional associations, and they can also reach out for collaboration with the ethnic professional associations. In addition, they may consider joining a consortium of organizations in their industry to jointly offer internships for people pursuing a particular line of work. The same networking measures taken to build relationships with feeder organizations when looking for experienced potential hires can also be used to identify diversity interns.

Here are some of the kinds of questions to formulate and answer as you begin expanding your outreach for diversity interns: Does your organization host meetings of National Association of Hispanic MBAs (NSHMBA), the National Association of Asian American Professionals, the Black Nurses Association, or similar organizations? Does someone from your organization actively participate in the professional and civic associations of people of color or people with disabilities? Do you recruit from historically black colleges, from colleges that have high populations of Native Americans, or from geographic areas with a large number of people from Spanish-speaking backgrounds? If not, it's time to start.

Essential for success in a diversity internship program is to carefully choose and train internship supervisors. This applies to all internship programs, and is not limited to those targeted for specific groups of young people of color. The personnel who will supervise the interns need to be individuals who have volunteered for the role. These supervisors need to be prepared to help the interns understand the big picture of the organization and the industry. They should have great coaching and feedback skills, be skilled at setting and monitoring performance standards, and have good networking skills. It is also important that they have knowledge of a range of learning styles. The internship experience needs to offer a substantive work experience related to the intern's major or field of interest. Finally, it is important that the internship supervisor has time built into his or her work schedule to provide attention, feedback and guidance to the intern.

Although internship supervisors do not need to be from a traditionally excluded group or have an identical cultural or racial background to that of their intern, it is important that the supervisor understand ways in which the intern's cultural values and worldview is different from their own. This can be accomplished through an orientation or development program that introduces supervisors to ways of working well with people who come from backgrounds or with life experience different than their own.

While some factual material on culture and values can be conveyed using web-based methods, at least part of their learning needs to take place in group learning sessions, including some form of diversity and inclusion workshop. Ideally, the learning experience will include interacting with individuals from a variety of backgrounds. It should include a focus on the particular concerns and life experience their diversity interns will bring with them. If the supervisors have not already had training to reduce bias when conducting interviews, this should be made available to them.

It is important that the supervisor come away with an understanding of behaviors, subtle and not-so-subtle, that contribute to an intern's feelings of inclusion or exclusion in the workplace. It is important that they acquire cultural lenses that will increase their understanding of the differences between people from group-oriented cultures and individual-oriented cultures, and high-context cultures and low-context cultures. These lenses will help the supervisor make sense of certain interns reactions that they might not have understood before, and can be useful when supervisors help their interns understand the culture and norms of the organization.

It will also be helpful for the supervisors to recognize the impact generational diversity can have on their dealings with their interns. In speaking of generations, we are not only talking about the differences between Boomers, X's, Y's and Millennials, but also about how people of a particular cultural group respond to the workplace and workplace supervision, depending on how many generations back their family arrived in this country. An awareness of when someone's family arrived in your area can help explain certain worldviews.

To better understand the generational diversity perspective, supervisors of diversity interns might ask themselves questions like: Is this Korean-American from the immigrant generation, and, if so, at what age did she come to this country? Was this Venezuelan intern born in the U.S.? Were her parents? Did this Chinese-American grow up in a Chinese-speaking household, or is he someone adopted into an English-speaking family? Did this young African-American man grow up in close-knit, rural Southern family? Is he part of the first generation to live in the North? What does "respect/disrespect" mean to this individual, and how is that expressed? Is this person a refugee or an immigrant?

Managers and supervisors can find the internship a valuable opportunity for mutual learning, both about workplace issues and about cultural differences. With this understanding they can better leverage the perspectives and address the learning needs of their interns of color, or their interns with disabilities.

The counterpart of supervisor training is a well-thought-out development program that is put in place for the interns themselves. It should have an orientation session – possibly the same one all new employees attend – and some group sessions to help these interns feel welcome in this workplace. In addition to the work projects given to the interns, they should have opportunities to meet a wide range of employees and have some contact with executive leadership. It should provide for coaching in workplace values and etiquette and provide them some introduction to the political dynamics of the workplace. Within that internship program there should be structured opportunities for the interns to meet together from time to time in homogeneous groups to compare their experiences and to learn from one another. It is also important for diversity interns to have exposure to staff who have a similar background to theirs.

There are already many internships reserved for students of color in finance, marketing, health care, engineering, computer science, journalism, accounting, Human Resources, the sciences and other fields. Organizations that offer diversity internships range from law firms to financial services firms to government agencies, pharmaceutical companies, publishers and health care organizations. Some well-known organizations with internships include IBM, Wyeth, Goldman Sachs, the Environmental Protection Agency, EMC, and JP Morgan Chase. Many companies have formed partnerships with Historically Black Colleges and Universities (HBCUs) and the United Negro College Fund to recruit not only African-American students, but also Hispanic students, Asian-American students and Native American students.

The National Hispanic Internship Program, which has been in business since 1992, is the largest Hispanic internship program and places interns primarily in federal agencies. There are paid and unpaid internships in many fields that are targeted for Asian-American and Pacific Islanders. Some internships are intended to attract more women to fields in which they are underrepresented.

For over 35 years, St. Louis-based InRoads has collaborated with hundreds of organizations across the US and Canada to identify and place interns of color. InRoads has a rigorous selection process; once interns are identified, they spend their college summers working in organizations affiliated with InRoads. Throughout each summer, they receive training sessions in business practices from InRoads staff and volunteers. During their multi-year internship experience, the students receive additional coaching and support during the school year from InRoads staff. Many go on to work for the company in which they interned.

Some internships are unfunded. Paid summer internships in organizations often range from $10,000-$15,000 and may convert to full-time employment when the student graduates. In setting up an inclusive internship program, it is important to look at what it will take to bring the talent you want to your table. In establishing a diversity internship program, are you prepared to put in place the extra supports that interns of non-traditional backgrounds may need? What are the creative ways you can facilitate diversity interns coming into a line of work that has not traditionally included people of their background?

In hosting a diversity internship your organization is introducing talented young people to hands-on opportunities in your line of work or your company. You are introducing them to your organizational culture and the culture of the modern workplace. You, in turn, have a great opportunity to set the next generation on the right path to workplace success while you get a wonderful window into the thinking patterns of today's young people of color. A well-run diversity internship program expands your organization's employee recruitment pipeline and contributes to a positive reputation for your products, services and employment prospects among not only the interns, but also the interns' friends, colleagues, and family.

If your company already has a program for diversity interns, Congratulations! If you already have a program, look for ways to enhance it. If you have not yet established a program for diversity interns, now is a good time to start!

Debora Bloom, M.A. and her company, Debora Bloom Associates, specialize in training and consulting services in the areas of workforce diversity, harassment prevention, and leadership development. Over the past 25 years, she has worked successfully with dozens of business, health care agencies, and government organizations on managing the human side of their business. She can be reached at DBloom@DBloomAssociates.com or 617-323-6566.

EMPLOYMENT LAW ISSUES FOR INTERNSHIPS[1]

Michael R. Brown
Partner, Seyfarth Shaw LLP

Internships have become a right of passage for college and university students. They are often viewed as the gateway to admission into more prestigious graduate schools and more financially rewarding employment. Many institutions of higher learning have incorporated internships into their undergraduate curriculum.[2] These internships provide students with practical experience and enhance the educational process. The explosion of student internships presents a host of potential employment law issues that are relatively new and have yet to be decided.

This section will discuss employment law issues for organizations that host student interns or internship programs. Its analysis will focus primarily on federal employment law issues, but will contain references to state law where applicable. It will highlight potential issues that organizations should be aware of and how they should structure their internship programs in such a fashion so as to decrease the potential likelihood for violating federal or state employment laws. However, it should be noted once again that this area of law is largely undecided, and it is difficult, if not impossible, to predict how a reviewing agency or court might rule on a particular internship program.[3]

Agreement

Employers often require employees to sign an employment agreement. This agreement establishes the particulars of employment, including compensation, sick pay, vacation pay, and duration of employment. Employees are often hired

---

[1] This chapter was prepared by Michael R. Brown, a Partner in the Boston office of Seyfarth Shaw LLP, who gratefully acknowledges the invaluable assistance of Vincent Domestico, a legal intern from Northeastern University Law School.

[2] For instance, both Northeastern University and Endicott College in the Boston, MA area make the successful completion of internships of varying lengths a requirement for graduation.

[3] In contrast to the uncertain nature of the legal landscape surrounding student internships programs, the reality is that, as internships become more important in the eyes of prospective employers, students realize that the short-term sacrifices (namely compensation) are outweighed by the long-term benefits. Accordingly, a student intern is unlikely to allege violations of employment statutes for fear of the damage that it might do to his/her professional aspirations. While an organization should not affirmatively fail to comply with federal and state employment laws, it should note that many of these laws fail to account for the realities of today's internships.

with the expectation that they will remain employed for a lengthy period of time. In contrast, student interns are usually engaged for a distinct period of time. These periods may range from a few weeks to many months. Must these employers have the school (if the internship is school-sponsored) or the intern sign an agreement establishing the terms and conditions of his/her engagement?

While agencies and courts have not ruled on this specific issue, it would appear to be good practice for an organization to have an agreement with the student intern and, in the case of institution-sponsored internships, with their school. This agreement should establish the parameters of the internship, and should also describe the degree of supervision the organization will have over the training and work of the student intern. It should also establish the expectation, or lack thereof, regarding the payment of wages and/or permanent employment.

University-sponsored internships have become increasingly common and popular in recent years. As mentioned earlier, some undergraduate and graduate institutions condition graduation upon the successful completion of multiple internships of varying lengths. It is likely that these internships will require greater supervision and evaluation than those that are not university-sponsored. Moreover, these agreements may specify the minimum number of hours a student is required to work, and minimum amount of wages a student intern must be paid. For instance, the agreement could require an intern to work for 35 hours per week, but forbid a host organization from requiring the student to work any more than 45 hours per week.

Employee vs. Volunteer

Is a paid student intern an "employee" of the organization hosting an internship program? Is an unpaid student intern an "employee" or "volunteer"? Does the intern attain a different status by virtue of the educational component of an internship program? It should be emphasized that the analysis of employee status varies depending upon the particular facts and circumstances of each potential situation. Also, the ultimate determination will depend in large part upon what federal or state employment law is being applied to the particular intern and the internship program.

For example, the U.S. Department of Labor (DOL) has established a six-part test to determine whether a student intern is an employee for the purposes of the Fair Labor Standards Act (FLSA).[4] Under this test, a student intern will

---

[4] While this test has been consistently applied by the DOL in its opinion letters and utilized by courts in wage and hour actions, it holds no precedential value. Moreover, this test is applicable to the employee status of an intern under the FLSA, and does not address any statewage and hour claims, workers' compensation claims, or other state employment issues.

not be considered an employee only if all of the following six factors are satisfied. The factors are: (1) the training, even though it includes actual operation of the facilities of the employer, is similar to that which would be given in a vocational school; (2) the training is for the benefit of the intern; (3) the interns do not displace regular employees, but work under their close observation; (4) the employer that provides the training receives no immediate advantage from the activities of the interns, and, on occasion, the operations may actually be impeded; (5) the interns are not necessarily entitled to a job at the conclusion of the training period; and (6) the employer and the interns understand that they are not entitled to wages for the time spent in training.

As noted earlier, the DOL has taken an all or nothing approach with respect to the application of its six part test. Thus, a student intern is an employee of the host organization unless the student satisfies each of the six criteria. The DOL has consistently stated (and some courts have agreed) that no single prong of the test is by itself dispositive. For example, the fact that a student intern and the host organization have an understanding that he or she is not entitled to a job at the completion of the internship does not preclude a finding of employee status. An employer must determine whether an internship satisfies each and every prong of the test. At the very least, a finding of "employee" status means the intern must be paid minimum wage and overtime.

Paid interns are almost always considered to be employees of the host organization because paid employment would not satisfy the sixth prong of the DOL's six part test (that the intern understands that he or she is not entitled to wages for the time spent in training). In contrast to the unpaid intern, the paid student intern accepts and works at the internship with the explicit understanding that he or she will be compensated for the time spent working for the host organization.[5]

The fourth prong of the DOL test provides that an intern cannot provide an employer with any immediate advantage or benefit. For instance, the DOL was asked in 1994 about an internship program assisting in the daily management of hostels. The DOL was asked whether the arrangement whereby students received a free room (approximately $15 a night) in exchange for 25 hours of work per week would violate the FLSA for failure to pay minimum wage to the students. The DOL stated "[b]ased on the information…it is our opinion that criterion number 4 discussed above would not be met, since it is apparent the employer derives an immediate advantage from the duties performed by the interns in question. Therefore, such interns would be considered

---

[5] Such a result could be particularly costly if the employer pays the student intern sub-minimum wage or fails to accurately compensate them for time spent working beyond forty hours per week.

employees under the FLSA and subject to its minimum wage and overtime pay provisions."[6]

A corollary to the fourth prong of the test is the third prong which precludes the intern from displacing regular employees. This prong of the test can be particularly troublesome for a host organization that relies heavily on its interns to do tasks that otherwise would fall to regular employees. An organization should be particularly careful if it readily admits or states that, without its interns, it would have to hire regular employees to do the jobs undertaken by interns. Such statements or actions will be sufficient to fail the fourth prong of the DOL test and therefore expose the employer to liability for violation of the FLSA.

Thus, an organization should pay particular attention to the third and fourth prongs of the DOL test. If it can be demonstrated that the employer gains an immediate benefit from the activities of the students, or if the intern displaces regular employees, the student will be an employee under the FLSA and thus subject to the wage and overtime laws contained therein. As noted earlier, it would be good practice to have the student intern sign an agreement acknowledging satisfaction of each prong of the DOL test. While this practice will not necessarily shield the hosting organization from liability under the FLSA, it will certainly strengthen the organization's defense against a potential FLSA violation assuming the acknowledgement is truthful. Additionally, the organization should emphasize to prospective interns in any application materials that they are not employees of the organization. Such language would serve to put the student on notice, and including such language in solicitation materials would alert the school about the classification.

Wage Issues

Student internship programs raise a number of issues regarding potential violations of wage and hour laws. The FLSA mandates employers to pay their employees a wage that is at least equivalent to the federal minimum wage. If the state minimum wage is higher than the federal minimum, the higher wage must be paid. In direct contrast to this requirement, a significant percentage of student internships are unpaid. Does having student interns work without receiving pay constitute a violation of the FLSA and other state wage and hour laws? Also, even if the host organization does not pay the student intern, are they nevertheless employees? An unpaid student intern clearly understands that they are not entitled to wages for the time spent in training. As noted earlier, student interns often provide immediate benefit to the host organization and

---

[6] Opinion Letter FLSA2004-5NA (May 17, 2004).

often displace regular employees. Thus, it is possible that an unpaid student intern may acquire employee status under the FLSA by virtue of their utility to the organization.

School-sponsored internship programs further muddy the waters, and make it increasingly difficult to determine whether an intern is an employee under the FLSA or state wage and hour laws. It is through this cloudy lense that an organization must look when assessing potential liability under state and federal wage and hour laws.

In 1996, the DOL was asked to determine the application of the FLSA to interns. While not specifically asked to address school-sponsored internship programs, the DOL nonetheless spoke to the issue in passing: "Where educational or training programs are designed to provide students with professional experience in the furtherance of their education and training is academically oriented for the benefit of the students, it is our position that the students will not be considered employees of the institution to which they are assigned, provided the six criteria [are] met." The DOL further addressed internships as a condition for graduation. It stated that "[i]n situations where students receive college credits applicable toward graduation when they volunteer to perform internships under a college program, and the program involves the students in real-life situations, and provides the students with educational experiences unobtainable in a classroom setting, we do not believe that an employment relationship exists between the students and the facility providing the instruction." This seemingly contradictory opinion letter states that student interns are not employees so long as they fulfill the six criteria, but at the same time students receiving credit are not employees. Obviously, this opinion does not provide clarity to a host organization and instead typifies the difficulty in classifying interns as employees or volunteers.

It is important to emphasize once again that states in which an organization is located may have differing tests for determining employee status under those states' wage and hour laws. Thus, it is crucial that an organization evaluate its jurisdiction's statutory and common law to determine whether interns are considered employees and therefore subject to state minimum wage and hour laws. For example, the Massachusetts Department of Labor (Mass. DOL) was called on to answer a related question.[7] The Mass. DOL replied "employment through the NU [Northeastern University] co-op program is work under a training program in an educational institution; therefore, it is not an 'occupa-

---

[7] Unfortunately the requesting organization asked the wrong question. Rather than asking whether co-op students were employees under Massachusetts wage and hour laws, it asked whether the student interns were professionals, and as such whether they were exempt from the Massachusetts Minimum Fair Wage Act.

tion' covered by the Massachusetts Fair Wage Law."[8] Unfortunately, the Mass. DOL did not, through its own initiative, answer the more important question for our purposes: is a student intern an employee for purposes of Massachusetts wage and hours laws? Nonetheless, the Mass. DOL's analysis appears to lean towards a finding of non-employee status for student interns. Thus, it is possible that the Mass. DOL (or other state DOL), would find that a school-sponsored program such as Northeastern's co-op program precludes a student intern from seeking protection under the Massachusetts wage and hour laws. Additionally, the Mass. DOL opinion letter does not address the impact of compensation in its analysis. The Mass. DOL's failure to address this issue does not clarify whether student interns are entitled to be paid minimum wage. As a result, it appears possible that an organization may compensate its student interns working under a school-sponsored internship program at a rate less than the Massachusetts minimum wage.

Workers Compensation

Another potential employment law issue regarding interns is whether they are employees for purposes of a state workers' compensation act.[9] For example, the Massachusetts Workers Compensation Act governs all workers' compensation claims and is the exclusive remedy for employees who suffer work related injuries. Thus, if under Massachusetts law the interns are employees, then they are covered under the Worker's Compensation Act. However, much as the employee/volunteer distinction was important under the FLSA, it is likewise crucial in determining the applicability of a state workers' compensation statute. If the interns are deemed to be volunteers, then they are not covered under a workers' compensation scheme and are not precluded from suing the organization for tort claims arising from their injuries sustained at work. This presents serious potential liability issues to host organizations, for many workers' compensation schemes limit employer liability.

For interns earning college credit or fulfilling graduation requirements, does the school's workers' compensation plan cover the student? While there is little case law and authority addressing this issue, a few courts have addressed the applicability of a workers' compensation statute to an intern for school credit.

---

[8] Opinion Letter MW-2001-017 (November 19, 2001)

[9] Workers' compensation is a matter of state law, and therefore this section will address selected workers' compensation statutes and cases involving student interns as examples only. This section should not be considered exhaustive, and it is encouraged that an organization determine whether an intern is covered under its workers' compensation policy or if an intern is covered under the school's policy.

For example, in one Colorado case[10] the court had to determine whether a paid student intern in a university-sponsored program was deemed an employee of the hosting organization for purposes of workers' compensation. The court held that the student was an employee of the organization for workers' compensation purposes and, moreover, that unpaid interns were also covered under the school's workers' compensation plan.

In a New York case,[11] the court addressed whether an unpaid student intern was covered under the school's workers' compensation plan. This court also held that the unpaid student intern was covered under the school's workers' compensation coverage, stating that where "necessary training and experience gained…is required for graduation and licensure, training is a thing of value and the equivalent of wages." While these cases are not dispositive on this issue, they do represent one avenue available to courts when confronted with these situations. As school-sponsored internships become more common, this issue will attract more court attention. While the answer is not fully clear, it is likely that a paid student intern will qualify as an employee under the various state workers' compensation acts, and that even unpaid interns may qualify under their schools' policies.

Vicarious Liability

May the actions of a student intern expose a host organization to liability? Vicarious liability may be imposed for the illegal acts of a company's employees committed within the course of their employment. Vicarious liability depends on whether the individual is an employee or independent contractor. While the law of each jurisdiction will vary, the law in Massachusetts, for example, would render most interns employees because internships tend to be highly supervised relationships. Thus, although an intern may not be considered an employee under the FLSA and Massachusetts wage and hour laws, that intern may nonetheless constitute an employee for liability purposes under state law.

Even if the interns do not constitute employees, an organization may be still be vicariously liable for negligence in selecting the intern or in directing the intern's work. For example, if an organization does not do any background check for an intern, it may be vicariously liable for its negligence in selection. This can be a particularly worrisome situation for financial institutions, health-care providers, or educational institutions hosting interns. Given the prevalence

---

[10] Kinder v. Industrial Claim Appeals Office, 976 P.2d 295, 1998 Colo. App. LEXIS 141, 27 Colo. Law. No. 7 219, 1998 Colo. J. C.A.R. 2729 (Colo. Ct. App. 1998)

[11] Olsson v. Nyack Hosp., 193 A.D.2d 1006, 598 N.Y.S.2d 348, 1993 N.Y. App. Div. LEXIS 5086 (N.Y. App. Div. 3d Dep't 1993)

of student internship programs, it is likely that an issue involving vicarious liability will arise in the near future. As of now, it is yet another unresolved area in the law involving student interns.

Discrimination Statutes

In light of the uncertain employment status of interns, may an intern nevertheless assert a federal or state discrimination claim against the host organization? For the one court that has addressed this issue, the answer is no.

In that case, [12] Bridget O'Connor was a student at a private college in New York. Her major in social work required her to perform 200 hours of field work at school-approved organizations. Her college arranged for her to be placed at Rockland (a hospital for the mentally disabled operated by the State of New York). As part of her practicum, O'Connor attended regular staff meetings and met with patients. She documented the results of her patient meetings to both her supervisor at Rockland and the faculty at her college. O'Connor was paid through a federal work study program for the time she spent at Rockland. Unfortunately for Ms. O'Connor, her experience at Rockland was not a pleasant one.

Within two days of starting her internship Ms. O'Connor had already been the subject of sexual harassment that only worsened over the following months. Ultimately, she left Rockland and her college arranged an internship at another organization. Subsequently, she filed suit against Rockland, claiming illegal sexual harassment under the federal discrimination laws. The court had to determine whether Ms. O'Connor was an employee within the meaning of these discrimination laws so that she would have standing to bring this case. The court dismissed her claims on the basis of her failure to satisfy the definition of employee.

Of particular importance to host organizations is the court's treatment of the unpaid nature of Ms. O'Connor's position. The court paid great attention to the lack of any remuneration that Ms. O'Connor received from Rockland: "As a volunteer, the plaintiff received no salary, no health benefits, retirement benefits, and also had no regular hours assigned…" As the court stated, "[w]e believe that the preliminary question of remuneration is dispositive in this case. It is uncontested that O'Connor received from Rockland no salary or other wages, and no employee benefits such as health insurance, vacation, or sick pay, nor was she promised any such compensation." Therefore, the court concluded that Ms. O'Connor could not bring a discrimination claim against Rockland because she was not an employee.

---

[12] O'Connor v. Davis, 126 F.3d 112, 1997 U.S. App. LEXIS 26401, 74 Fair Empl. Prac. Cas. (BNA) 1561 (2d Cir. N.Y. 1997)

Summary

While internships of all kinds have become more popular, there are many legal issues that are still unanswered. Until we have more answers, a hosting organization should be aware of the distinct likelihood that an intern will be considered an employee under federal law – and thus should be paid minimum wage and overtime. In addition, an intern will most likely be eligible for workers' compensation if injured on the job, and could impose vicarious liability on the host organization. As noted, these issues and others are subject to both federal law and the law of the state of the host organization. Hopefully, there will be more definitive answers in the years to come.

Michael Brown has advised employers in all aspects of labor and employment law for over 40 years. He is a Senior Partner in the Boston office of Seyfarth Shaw LLP. His telephone number is 617-946-4907 and his email address is mrbrown@seyfarth.com.

APPENDIX

APPENDIX A
LIST OF MAJORS

Agriculture & Related Sciences

Agribusiness Operations

Agricultural Business

Agricultural Business Technology

Agricultural Communications

Agricultural Economics

Agricultural Education Services

Agricultural Equipment Technology

Agricultural Mechanization

Agricultural Power Machinery

Agricultural Production

Agricultural Supplies

Agricultural/Food Processing

Agriculture - General

Agronomy/Crop Science

Animal Breeding

Animal Grooming

Animal Health

Animal Husbandry

Animal Nutrition

Animal Sciences

Animal Training

Aquaculture

Crop Production

Dairy Husbandry/Production

Dairy Science

International Agriculture

Landscaping

Livestock Management

Pest Management

Plant Breeding

Plant Sciences

Plant/Nursery Operations

Poultry Science

Range Science/Management

Soil Science and Agronomy

Taxidermy

Turf Management

Architecture & Related Programs

Architectural History/Criticism

Architectural Technology

Architecture

Architecture
    & Related Programs - General

City/Community/Regional Planning

Environmental Design

Interior Architecture

Landscape Architecture

Area, Ethnic, Cultural, & Gender Studies

African Studies
African-American Studies
American Studies
Area Studies
Asian American Studies
Asian Studies
Canadian Studies
Caribbean Studies
Central/Eastern European Studies
Chinese Studies
East Asian Studies
European Studies
French Studies
Gay/Lesbian Studies
German Studies
Hispanic-American Studies
Italian Studies
Japanese Studies
Korean Studies
Latin American Studies
Native American Studies
Near/Middle Eastern Studies
Pacific Area/Near Rim Studies
Polish Studies
Regional Studies
Russian/Slavic Area Studies
Scandinavian Area Studies

Slavic Studies
South Asian Studies
Southeast Asian Studies
Spanish/Iberian Studies
Ural-Altaic/Central Asian Studies
Western European Studies
Women's Studies

Arts, Visual & Performing

Acting
Art - General
Art History / Criticism / Conservation
Arts - General
Arts Management
Ballet
Ceramics
Commercial Photography
Commercial/Advertising Art
Crafts/Folk Art/Artisanry
Dance
Design/Visual Communications
Directing/Theatrical Production
Drama/Theater Arts
Drawing
Fashion Design
Fiber/Textile/Weaving Arts
Film Production/Cinematography
Film Studies
Fine/Studio Arts

Total Internship Management

Graphic Design	**Biological & Biomedical Sciences**
Illustration	Anatomy
Industrial Design	Animal Behavior/Ethology
Interior Design	Animal Genetics
Jazz Studies	Animal Physiology
Metal/Jewelry Arts	Aquatic Biology/Limnology
Multimedia	Bacteriology
Music - General	Biochemistry
Music - General Performance	Bioinformatics
Music - Piano/Organ	Biological Immunology
Music - Voice/Opera	Biology
Music Conducting	Biomedical Sciences
Music History/Literature	Biometrics
Music Management/Merchandising	Biophysics
Music Pedagogy	Biostatistics
Music Theory/Composition	Biotechnology
Musicology/Ethnomusicology	Botany
Painting	Cellular Biology/Histology
Photography	Cellular/Anatomical Biology
Playwriting/Screenwriting	Cellular/Molecular Biology
Printmaking	Chemical/Physical/Molecular Biology
Sculpture	Conservation Biology
Stringed Instruments	Developmental Biology/Embryology
Theater Design/Stagecraft	Ecology
Theater Literature/History/Criticism	Entomology
Theatre Arts Management	Environmental Biology
	Environmental Toxicology
	Epidemiology
	Evolutionary Biology

Exercise Physiology	**Business, Management, & Marketing**
Genetics	Accounting
Genetics - Human/Medical	Accounting Technology
Marine/Aquatic Biology	Accounting/Business Management
Microbiology	Accounting/Finance
Molecular Biochemistry	Actuarial Science
Molecular Biology	Administrative/Secretarial Services
Molecular Genetics	Apparel/Accessories Marketing
Molecular Pharmacology	Auctioneering
Neuroanatomy	Auditing
Neurobiology/Physiology	Banking/Financial Services
Oncology	Business - General
Parasitology	Business Administration/Management
Pathology - Human/Animal	Business Communications
Pharmacology	Business Statistics
Pharmacology/Toxicology	Business/Managerial Economics
Physiology	Construction Management
Plant Genetics	Credit Management
Plant Molecular Biology	Customer Service Management
Plant Pathology	Customer Service Support
Plant Physiology	E-Commerce
Radiation Biology	Entrepreneurial Studies
Reproductive Biology	Executive Assistant
Systematic Biology	Fashion Merchandising
Toxicology	Finance/Banking
Wildlife Biology	Financial Planning
Zoology	Financial Services Marketing
	Franchising Operations

Total Internship Management

Hospitality Administration
    & Management
Hospitality/Recreation Marketing
Hotel/Motel Management
Human Resources Development
Human Resources Management
Information Processing/Data Entry
Information Resources Management
Insurance/Risk Management
International Business
International Finance
International Marketing
Investments/Securities
Knowledge Management
Labor Studies
Labor/Personnel Relations
Logistics/Materials Management
Management Information Systems
Management Science
Marketing Management
Marketing Research
Merchandising
Nonprofit Management
Office Clerical Services
Office Management
Operations Management
Organizational Behavior Studies
Personal/Financial Services Marketing
Public Finance

Purchasing / Procurement / Contracts
Real Estate
Reception
Resort Management
Restaurant/Food Services
    Management
Retailing
Sales and Distribution
Sales/Selling Skills
Small Business Administration
Special Products Marketing
Taxation
Tourism/Travel Marketing
Tourism/Travel Services
Transportation/Transportation
    Management
Travel/Tourism Management
Vehicle Parts/Accessories Marketing
Warehousing/Inventory Management

Communications & Journalism

Advertising
Broadcast Journalism
Communications/Rhetoric
Digital Communications/Multimedia
Health Communications
Journalism
Mass Communications/Media Studies
Organizational Communication

Photojournalism

Political Communications

Public Relations

Publishing

Radio/Television

Communications Technologies

Animation/Special Effects

Communications Technologies - General

Computer Typography

Desktop Publishing

Graphic Communications

Graphic/Printing Equipment Operation

Photographic/Film Technology

Platemaking

Printing Management

Printing Press Operations

Radio/Television Broadcasting

Recording Arts Technology

Computer & Information Sciences

Artificial Intelligence/Robotics

Computer Graphics

Computer Networking/ Telecommunications

Computer Programming - General

Computer Programming - Specific Application

Computer Programming - Vendor/Product Certification

Computer Science

Computer Systems Analysis

Computer/Information Sciences - General

Computer/Systems Security

Data Entry Applications

Data Processing Technology

Database Management

Information Sciences/Systems

Information Technology

Networking/LAN/WAN Management

System Administration

Web/Multimedia Design

Web/Multimedia Management

Word Processing

Construction Trades

Building Construction Inspection

Building/Property Maintenance

Carpentry

Concrete Finishing

Construction Site Management

Construction Trades - General

Drywall Installation

Electrician

Metal Building Assembly

Painting/Wall Covering

Pipefitting

Plumbing

Power/Electric Transmission

Roofing

Well Drilling

Education

Adult Literacy Instruction

Adult/Continuing
   Education Administration

Adult/Continuing Teacher Education

Agricultural Education

Art Teacher Education

Bilingual/Bicultural Education

Biology Teacher Education

Business Teacher Education

Chemistry Teacher Education

College Counseling

Computer Teacher Education

Counselor Education

Curriculum/Instruction

Drama/Dance Teacher Education

Driver/Safety Education

ESL Teacher Education

Early Childhood Education

Early Childhood Special Education

Education - General

Education Administration/Supervision

Education of Blind/
   Visually Handicapped

Education of Brain Injured

Education of Deaf/Hearing Impaired

Education of Developmentally
   Delayed

Education of Emotionally
   Handicapped

Education of Gifted/Talented

Education of Learning Disabled

Education of Mentally Handicapped

Education of Multiple Handicapped

Education of Physically Handicapped

Education of Speech Impaired

Education of the Autistic

Educational Assessment/Testing

Educational Evaluation/Research

Educational Statistics/Research Methods

Elementary Education

English Teacher Education

Family/Consumer Sciences - Education

Foreign Language Teacher Education

French Teacher Education

French as Second/Foreign Language

Geography Teacher Education

German Teacher Education

Health Occupations
   Teacher Education

Health Teacher Education

History Teacher Education

Instructional Media

International/Comparative Education

Junior High Education

Kindergarten/Preschool Education

Latin Teacher Education

Mathematics Education

Montessori Teacher Education

Multicultural Education

Music Teacher Education

Native American Education

Physical Education

Physics Teacher Education

Psychology Teacher Education

Reading Teacher Education

Sales/Marketing Education

School Librarian Education

Science Teacher Education

Secondary Education

Social Science Teacher Education

Social Studies Teacher Education

Social/Philosophical
    Foundations of Education

Spanish Language Teacher Education

Special Education

Speech Teacher Education

Teacher Assistance

Teacher Education, Multiple Levels

Technology/Industrial Arts Education

Trade/Industrial Education

Waldorf/Steiner Teacher Education

Engineering

Aeronautical/Aerospace Engineering

Agricultural Engineering

Architectural Engineering

Biomedical Engineering

Ceramic Sciences/Engineering

Chemical Engineering

Civil Engineering

Computer Engineering - General

Computer Hardware Engineering

Construction Engineering

Electrical/Communications
    Engineering

Engineering - General

Engineering Mechanics

Engineering Physics

Engineering Science

Environmental Engineering

Forest Engineering

Geological Engineering

Geotechnical Engineering

Industrial Engineering

Manufacturing Engineering

Marine Engineering/
    Naval Architecture

147

Total Internship Management

Materials Engineering

Materials Science

Mechanical Engineering

Metallurgical Engineering

Mining/Mineral Engineering

Nuclear Engineering

Ocean Engineering

Operations Research

Petroleum

Polymer/Plastics

Software Engineering

Structural Engineering

Surveying Engineering

Systems Engineering

Textile Sciences/Engineering

Water Resource Engineering

Engineering Technologics

Aeronautical/Aerospace Engineering

Architectural Drafting

Architectural Engineering Technology

Automotive Engineering Technology

Biomedical Engineering Technology

CAD/CADD Drafting/Design

Civil Drafting/Civil Engineering

Civil Engineering/Technology

Computer Engineering

Computer Hardware

Computer Software

Computer Systems

Construction/Building Technologies

Drafting and Design Technology

Electrical Engineering Technologies

Electrical/Electronics Drafting

Electromechanical Technologies

Energy Systems

Engineering Technology - General

Engineering/Industrial Management

Environmental Engineering
    Technology

Hazardous Materials Management

Heating/A.C./Refrigeration

Hydraulics/Fluid Power

Industrial Safety

Industrial Technology

Instrumentation Technology

Laser/Optical Technology

Manufacturing Technologies

Mechanical Drafting

Metallurgical Technology

Mining

Nuclear

Occupational Safety

Petroleum Technology

Plastics

Quality Control

Robotics

Solar Energy

Surveying Technology

Telecommunications

Water Quality/Treatment

English Language & Literature

American Literature

American Literature (Canadian)

Creative Writing

English

English Composition

English Language; Literature - General

English Literature (British)

Speech/Rhetorical Studies

Technical/Business Writing

Family & Consumer Sciences

Adult Development/Aging

Apparel/Textile Manufacturing

Apparel/Textile Marketing Management

Child Care Management

Child Care Service

Child Development

Clothing/Apparel/Textile Studies

Consumer Economics

Consumer Merchandising

Consumer Services/Advocacy

Facilities/Event Planning

Family Resource Management Studies

Family Systems

Family/Community Services

Fashion/Fabric Consultant

Foods/Nutrition Studies

Family/Consumer Sciences - General

Family/Consumer Sciences - Business

Home Furnishings

Housing Studies

Human Development/Family Studies

Human Nutrition

Human Sciences Communication

Institutional Food Production

Textile Science

Work/Family Studies

Foreign Language & Literature

African

American Sign Language (ASL)

Ancient Near Eastern/ Biblical Languages

Arabic

Celtic

Chinese

Classics

Comparative Literature

Czech

Danish

Dutch/Flemish

East Asian

Filipino/Tagalog

Foreign Language; Literature -
    General

French

German

Germanic Languages

Greek, Ancient

Greek, Modern

Hebrew

Iranian/Persian

Italian

Japanese

Korean

Language Interpretation/Translation

Latin

Linguistics

Native American

Norwegian

Polish

Portuguese

Romance Languages

Russian

Sanskrit/Classical Indian

Scandinavian

Semitic

Sign Language Interpretation

Slavic

South Asian

Southeast Asian

Spanish

Swedish

Turkish

Ukrainian

Urdu

Health Professions & Clinical Sciences

Acupuncture

Anesthesiologist Assistant

Art Therapy

Asian Bodywork Therapy

Athletic Training/Sports Medicine

Audiology/Hearing Sciences

Bioethics/Medical Ethics

Cardiopulmonary Technology

Cardiovascular Technology

Chinese Medicine/Herbology

Chiropractic Assistant

Clinical Laboratory Science

Clinical Nutrition

Clinical Pastoral Counseling

Clinical/Medical Laboratory
    Technology

Clinical/Medical Social Work

Communication Disorders

Community Health Services

Community Health/
    Preventative Medicine

Cytogenetics Technology

Cytotechnology

Dance Therapy

Dental Assistance

Dental Hygiene

Dental Laboratory Technology

Diagnostic Medical Sonography

Dietetic Technician

Dietician Assistant

EMT Ambulance Attendant

Electrocardiograph Technology

Electroencephalograph Technology

Emergency Medical Technology

Environmental Health

Gene Therapy

Genetic Counseling

Health Aide

Health Facilities Administration

Health Physics/Radiologic Health

Health Services - General

Health Services Administration

Health System Administration

Hematology Technology

Herbalism

Histologic Technician

Histologic Technology

Home Attendant

Homeopathic Medicine

Kinesiotherapy

Management/Clinical Assistant

Marriage/Family Therapy

Massage Therapy

Maternal/Child Health

Medical Administrative Assistance

Medical Assistance

Medical Claims Examiner

Medical Dietetics

Medical Illustrating

Medical Informatics

Medical Insurance Billing

Medical Insurance Coding

Medical Laboratory Assistance

Medical Office Administration

Medical Office Assistant

Medical Office Computer Specialist

Medical Radiologic Technology

Medical Reception

Medical Records Administration

Medical Records Technology

Medical Staff Services Technology

Medical Transcription

Medication Aide

Medicinal/Pharmaceutical Chemistry

Mental Health Counseling

Mental Health Services Technology

Midwifery

Total Internship Management

Movement Therapy/Education

Music Therapy

Nuclear Medical Technology

Nursing (RN)

Nursing - Adult Health

Nursing - Critical Care

Nursing - Family Practice

Nursing - Maternal/Child Health

Nursing - Occupational/Environmental Health

Nursing - Pediatric

Nursing - Practical

Nursing - Preoperative/Surgical

Nursing - Psychiatric

Nursing - Public Health

Nursing Administration

Nursing Anesthesiology

Nursing Assistance

Nursing Midwifery

Nursing Science

Occupational Health/ Industrial Hygiene

Occupational Therapy

Occupational Therapy Assistance

Ophthalmic Laboratory Technology

Ophthalmic Technology

Opticianry/Opthalmic Dispensing Service

Optometric Technician/Assistant

Orthotics/Prosthetics

Pathology Assistant

Perfusion Technology

Pharmacy Assistance

Phlebotomy

Physical Therapy

Physical Therapy Assistance

Physician Assistance

Pre-Dentistry

Pre-Medicine

Pre-Nursing

Pre-Pharmacy

Pre-Veterinary Medicine

Public Health

Public Health Education

Radiation Protection Technician

Radiologic Technology/ Medical Imaging

Recreational Therapy

Renal/Dialysis Technology

Respiratory Therapy

Respiratory Therapy Technician

Speech-Language Pathology

Speech-Language Pathology/ Audiology

Substance Abuse Counseling

Surgical Technology

Veterinarian Assistance

Vocational Rehabilitation Counseling

Ward Clerk

Yoga Therapy/Teacher Training

History

American History (U.S.)

Asian History

Canadian History

European History

History - General

History of Science/Technology

Public History/Archives

Law & Legal Studies

Court Reporting

Legal Administrative Assistance

Paralegal/Legal Assistance

Pre-Law

Liberal Arts & Sciences

General Studies

Humanities

Liberal Arts; Sciences

Library Science

Library Assistance

Library Science

Mathematics

Algebra/Number Theory

Analysis/Functional Analysis

Applied Mathematics

Computational Mathematics

Mathematics - General

Statistics

Statistics/Probability

Mechanic & Repair Technologies

Aircraft Mechanics

Aircraft Powerplant Technology

Alternative Fuel Vehicle Technology

Appliance Installation/Repair

Auto Body Repair

Automotive Technology

Avionics Maintenance/Technology

Business Machine Repair

Communications Systems

Computer Installation/Repair

Diesel Mechanics

Electrical/Electronics
      Equipment Repair

Engine Machinist

Gunsmithing

Heating/A.C./Refrigeration
      Mechanics

Heavy Equipment Maintenance

Industrial Electronics

Industrial Equipment
      Maintenance/Repair

Locksmithing

Marine Maintenance/Ship Repair

Mechanics; Repair - General

Medium/Heavy Vehicle Technology

Motorcycle Maintenance/Repair

Musical Instrument
   Fabrication/Repair

Security Systems

Small Engine Mechanics/Repair

Vehicle Emissions
   Inspection/Maintenance

Watchmaking/Jewelrymaking

Multi/Interdisciplinary Studies

Accounting/Computer Science

Ancient Studies/Civilization

Behavioral Sciences

Biological/Physical Sciences

Biopsychology

Classical/Ancient Mediterranean/
   Near Eastern Studies

Cognitive Science

Cultural Resource Management

Gerontology

Global Studies

Historic Preservation/Conservation

Intercultural/Multicultural/
   Diversity Studies

Mathematics/Computer Science

Medieval/Renaissance Studies

Museum Studies

Natural Sciences

Neuroscience

Nutrition Sciences

Peace/Conflict Resolution Studies

Science, Technology; Society

Systems Science/Theory

Natural Resources & Conservation

Environmental Science

Environmental Studies

Fishing/Fisheries

Forest Management

Forest Resources Production

Forest Sciences/Biology

Forest Technology

Forestry - General

Land Use Planning

Natural Resource Economics

Natural Resources; Conservation -
   General

Natural Resources
   Management/Policy

Urban Forestry

Water/Wetlands/Marine Management

Wildlife/Wilderness Management

Wood Science/Paper Technology

Parks, Recreation & Fitness

Exercise Sciences

Health/Physical Fitness

Parks, Recreation, Fitness - General

Parks/Leisure Facilities Management

Sport/Fitness Administration

Personal & Culinary Services

Aesthetics/Skin Care

Baking/Pastry Arts

Barbering

Bartending

Beauty Salon Management

Cosmetic Services

Cosmetology

Culinary Arts/Chef Training

Culinary Arts/Related Services

Facial Treatments

Food Prep/Professional Cooking

Food Service

Funeral Direction

Funeral Services/Mortuary Science

Hair Styling/Design

Institutional Food Service

Make-up

Manicure/Nails

Mortuary Science/Embalming

Personal; Culinary Services - General

Restaurant/Catering Management

Philosophy & Religion

Buddhist Studies

Christian Studies

Ethics

Islamic Studies

Jewish/Judaic Studies

Logic

Philosophy

Philosophy; Religion - General

Religion/Religious Studies

Physical Sciences

Acoustics

Analytical Chemistry

Astronomy

Astrophysics

Atmospheric Physics Dynamics

Atmospheric Sciences

Atomic/Molecular Physics

Chemical Physics

Chemistry

Geochemistry

Geology

Geophysics Seismology

Hydrology Water Resources

Inorganic Chemistry

Meteorology

Oceanography

Optics

Organic Chemistry

Paleontology

Physical Sciences - General

Physical Theoretical Chemistry

Physics

Planetary Sciences

Polymer Chemistry

Theoretical Mathematical Physics

Precision Production Trades

Boilermaking

Cabinetmaking Millwork

Furniture Design Manufacturing

Ironworking

Machine Shop Technology

Machine Tool Technology

Precision Production Trades - General

Sheet Metal Technology

Shoe/Boot/Leather Repair

Tool/Die Technology

Upholstery

Welding Technology

Woodworking

Psychology

Clinical Psychology

Community Psychology

Counseling Psychology

Developmental/Child Psychology

Educational Psychology

Experimental Psychology

Family Psychology

Forensic Psychology

Industrial/Organizational Psychology

Personality Psychology

Psychobiology/Physiological
  Psychology

Psychology - General

Social Psychology

Public Administration & Services

Community Organization/Advocacy

Human Services

Public Administration

Public Policy Analysis

Public Services

Social Work

Youth Services

Science Technologies

Biology Technician

Chemical Technology

Industrial Radiologic Technology

Nuclear Power Technology

Science Technologies

Security & Protective Services

Correctional Facilities Administration

Corrections
Criminal Justice Studies
Criminalistics/Criminal Science
Fire Protection/Safety Technology
Fire Science/Firefighting
Fire Services Administration
Forensic Technologies
Juvenile Corrections
Law Enforcement Administration
Police Science
Protective Services
Security Services Management
Security/Loss Prevention

Social Sciences

American Government/Politics
Anthropology
Applied Economics
Archaeology
Canadian Government/Politics
Cartography
Criminology
Demography/Population Studies
Development Economics
Econometrics
Economics
Geography
International Economics
International Relations

International Relations
Political Science/Government
Social Sciences - General
Sociology
Urban Studies

Theological Studies &
Religious Vocations

Bible Studies
Ministry
Missionary Studies
Pastoral Counseling
Pre-Ministerial Studies
Religious Education
Religious/Sacred Music
Talmudic Studies
Theology
Youth Ministry

Transportation &
Materials Moving

Air Traffic Control
Air Transportation
Airline - Commercial Pilot/
   Flight Crew
Aviation Management
Commercial Fishing
Construction/Earthmoving
   Equipment

Total Internship Management

Diving - Professional/Instruction

Flight Attendance

Flight Instruction

Marine Science/Merchant Marines

Transportation &
Materials Moving - General

Truck/Bus/Commercial
Vehicle Operation

Source: "Major and Career Profiles" Copyright (c) 2007 The College Board, www.collegeboard.com. Reproduced with permission.

APPENDIX B
SAMPLE LIST OF STUDENT CLUBS

The list below represents a collection of clubs and organizations at Boston University. Not all of the clubs listed here are available at all institutions. Likewise, most institutions will have organizations not listed here. This section of the appendix provides a preliminary resource in building a foundational understanding of the vast number, and different types, of student organizations on today's college campuses

Community Service Organizations

Organization Name

Alpha Phi Omega

AWARE

Building Tomorrow

Campus Girl Scouts

Child at Heart

China Care Fund

COM Champions

Dance Marathon

Darfur Coalition

Engineers Without Borders

Environmental Student Organization

Exposure Initiative

Fight JPA

First Book Campus Advisory Board

Foundation of International Medical
    Relief of Children

Free The Children Campus Initiative

Global Alliance to
    Immunize Against Aids

Global Medical Brigades

H.A.V.E. (Hunger Affects
    Virtually Everyone)

Habitat for Humanity International

Heartbeat Africa

Hug Don't Hate

International Student Volunteers

ONE

Peer Health Exchange

Red Cross Volunteers

Rotaract

Silver Wings

Speak Easy

Students for Camp Heartland

Students Infecting the Community
    with Kindness

UNICEF Campus Initiative

Unite for Sight

Culture Organizations

African Students Organization

Total Internship Management

Albanian Club

Arab Students Association

Armenian Students Association

Asian Student Union

Asian Studies Initiative

Asociacion de Estudiantes
    Graduados de Espanol

Bangladeshi Students' Association

Bhangra

Brazilian Association

BU PorColombia

Chinese Student and
    Scholar Association

Chinese Students Association

Cuban-American Student Association

Danzon

Filipino Student Association

French Cultural Society

Hawaii Cultural Association

Hellenic Association

Hillel Students Organization

Hong Kong Student Association

India Club

Indonesian Society

International Student Hospitality Association

International Students Consortium

Italian Students Association

Japanese Student Association

Kalaniot

Korean Student Association

La Fuerza

Latinos Unidos

Lebanese Club

Mexican Student Association

Organization of
    Pakistani Students

Palestinian - Israeli
    Peace Alliance

Persian Student Cultural Club

Polish Society

Preservation of Endangered
    Cultures Project

Russian Cultural Society

Singapore Society

Spectrum

Spice

Students for Israel

Taiwanese American
    Student Association

Taiwanese Student Association

TARANG Indian
    Student's Association

Thai Students Association

Turkish Student Association

Undergraduate Chinese Society

UMOJA

Vietnamese Student Association

Law Organizations

American Civil Liberties Union -
   LAW

American Constitution Society

Asian Pacific American
   Law Students Association

Black Law Students Association

BUSL Coffeehouse

Children and the Law

Communication, Entertainment,
   Sports Law Assn.

Earthrights International - LAW

Environmental Law Society

Federalist Society

Health Law Association

Intellectual Property Law Society

International Law Society

IP Society Student Bar Association

J. Reuben Clark Law Society

Jewish Law Students Association

Labor & Employment Law

Latin American Law
   Student Association

LAW Softball Team

Law Students for Choice

Legal Follies

Older Wiser Law Students

OutLaw

Phi Alpha Delta

Public Interest Project

Shelter Legal Services

South Asian American
   Law Students Association

Student Government LAW School

Women's Law Association

Performance Organizations

Allegrettos

Athena's Players

Aural Fixation

Ballroom Dance

Barbershop Sweethearts

Boston Lindy Kats

BosTones, The

BU Band

BU On Tap

Bulletproof Funk

Capoeira Club

Chankaar

Choral Society

Chordially Yours

Composers and Musicians

Concert Band

Dance Theatre Group

Dear Abbeys

Dheem: Classical Indian
   Dance Association

Edge, The

Total Internship Management

Encore!

Exhibition Drill Team

Fusion

Garba/Raas Club

Giddha

In Achord

Jalwa

Jazz Band

Liquid Fun

Marching Band

On Broadway

Orchestra

Outtakes, The

Pep Band

Record Label

Shakespeare Society

Slow Children At Play

Soulstice

Speak for Yourself

Stage Troupe

Step About Boston

Suno (Hindi A Cappella)

Sweet Liberty Dance Team

Terpsichore

TFE (Theater for Engineers)

Treblemakers

Trú Sole

Underground Music Appreciation

Unofficial Project

Vibes

Wandering Minds

Willing Suspension

Political Organizations

American Civil Liberties Union - Undergraduate

Americans for Informed Democracy

Amnesty International

College Democrats

College Republicans

Debate Society

Friends of Spartacus Youth

International Relations Organization

Libertarian Society

Liberty in North Korea

Model United Nations

NAACP

Right to Life

Students Against Human Trafficking

Students for a Democratic Society

Students for MASS PIRG

Unity 08 College Team

US India Political Action Committee

VOX: Voices for Choices

Women's Center

World Affairs Forum

Professional Organizations

Ad Club

Alpha Epsilon Delta

Alpha Eta Mu Beta Honor Society

Alpha Kappa Psi

Alpha Sigma Lambda

American Institute of
    Aeronautics & Astronautics

American Marketing Association

American Society of
    Mechanical Engineers (ASME)

Anthro Works

Archaeology Club

Arnold Air Society

Art History Association

Art League

Arts Administration
    Student Association

Astronomical Society

Beta Alpha Psi

Bioethics Society

Biomedical Engineers Society

Biotechnology Association

BSBA Private Equity

CAS Dean's Host

Chemia

Club Managers of America

Creative Writing Club

Deaf Studies Club

Delta Sigma Pi

Diner's Club

Diversity in Management

Early Childhood Educators Club

Editorial Society

Elementary Education

Entrepreneurship Club

Environmental Examiner

Eta Kappa Nu

Exceptional Educators

Fashion and Retail Association

Fine Arts Management
    & Education Society

First Draft

FIRST Robotics

Geological Society

Golden Key Honor Society

Growling Dog Productions

Health Science Club

Human Physiology Society

Institute of Electrical
    & Electronics Engineers

Institute of Industrial Engineers

International Management
    Organization

Kappa Kappa Psi

Korean Business Club

Leaders for Corporate
    Social Responsibility

Total Internship Management

Linguistics Association

Lock Honorary Service Society

Management Consulting Association

Management of
Information Systems Club

Marine Science Association

Mathletic Association

Mathematical Association of America

Media and Entertainment Club

Minorities in Law

Minority Association
of Pre-Health Students

Minority Engineers Society

Mock Trial Organization

Motion Picture Association

Music Educators
National Conference

National Society for
Minorities in Hospitality

National Society
of Collegiate Scholars

National Student Speech Language
Hearing Assn

Nutrition Club

Occupational Therapy Club

Operations Management

Physical Therapy Association

Pi Sigma Alpha

Pi Tau Sigm

Pre Dental Society

Pre Law Review

Pre Law Society

Pre Medical Society

Pre Veterinary Society

Pre-Med Study Assistance

Pre-Optometry Professional Society

Psi Chi

Public Health Initiative

Public Relations Student
Society of America

Real Estate Club

Rehabilitation Counselors
Organization

Rocket Team

Sargent College Honor Society

Sigma Alpha Lambda

SMG Pre Law Society

Society of Athletic Training Students

Society of Automotive Engineers

Society of Hispanic
Professional Engineers

Society of Professional Journalists

Society of Women Engineers

Sports Management Association

Students for the Development &
Advancement of Higher Education

Tau Beta Pi Association

Tau Beta Sigma

Undergraduate Classics Association

Undergraduate Economics
Association

Undergraduate History Association

Undergraduate Mathematics
Association

Undergraduate Philosophy
Association

Undergraduate Psychology
Association

Undergraduate Religion Association

Venture Capital Private Equity

Writer's Workshop

Recreation Organizations

Alpine Ski Team

Badminton Club

Baseball Club

Cheerleading Squad

Cycling

Dance Team

Equestrian Team

Fencing Club

Gymnastics Club

Inline Hockey Team

Kung Fu Club

Men's Lacrosse

Men's Rugby Club

Men's Volleyball Club

Men's Water Polo

Shotokan Karate Club

Snowboard Team

Submission Grappling

Synchronized Skating Team

Synchronized Swimming

Table Tennis Association

Ultimate Frisbee

Women's Rugby Club

Women's Volleyball Club

Religious Organizations

Asian American Christian Fellowship

Asian Baptist Student Koinonia

Baha'i Association

Buddhist Association

Chabad Jewish Student Organization

Chi Alpha Christian Fellowship

Christians on Campus

Episcopal Student Organization

Hindu Students Council

Hong Kong Students
Christian Fellowship

Inner Strength Gospel Choir

Intervarsity Christian Fellowship

Islamic Society

Latter-day Saint Student Association

Lotus: Buddhist Club

Lutheran Campus Ministry

Milahl: Korean
    Christian Fellowship

Mustard Seed

Navigators Christian Fellowship

Nemeton: Wiccan
    Student Alliance

Orthodox Christian Fellowship

Real Life: Campus Crusade
    for Christ

Sikh Association

Unitarian Universalist
    Campus Organization

Victory Campus Ministry

Vita Novis Christian Fellowship

Women's Interfaith Action Group

Social Organizations

Ages 8 & Up

Anime Group

Art Proliferation Society

Billiards Club

Boston Scholars Club

Bowling Association

Brownstone Journal

BURN Magazine

Chess Club

Cigar Aficionado Society

Club Domestique

College Bowl

Cricket Club

Crud Curling Club

DDR

Drink Responsibly

Film Society

Flintknapping Club

Holocaust
    Education Committee

Juggling Association

Knitting Club

Literary Society

Mac Users Group

Massively-Multiplayer
    Online Gaming Society

Medieval Recreation Society

Organic Gardening Club

Origami Club

Outing Club

Photography Club

Role-Playing Society

SAR: Class of 2007

SAR: Class of 2008

Scuba Divers

Ski & Snowboard Club

Students for
    Sensible Drug Policy

Students in Free Enterprise

Tennis Club

Transitional Mentor Program

Triathletes and Beyond	Society
Video Game	Zen Society

Printed with permission from the Boston University Student Activities Office.

APPENDIX C
SAMPLE INTERVIEW QUESTIONS

The following represent the questions, as reported by employers, that organizations are most likely to ask in an internship interview.

- What kind of realistic commitment to work hours can you make?
- What are you looking to get out of this experience?
- How has your college education provided you with the tools necessary to follow your career path?
- Why are you interested in this opportunity?
- Why have you chosen our organization to intern with?
- What are your expectations of this internship?
- What is your expectation of being guided by supervisors?
- Why are you looking to complete an internship?
- What are your goals after graduation?
- Where do you see yourself in three to five years, and how do you see yourself getting there?
- You may be asked to complete some mundane assignments, such as filing – how do you feel about this?
- How do you plan on applying your classroom education to this internship?
- What is your idea of the ideal internship?
- How does our mission statement resonate with you?

The remaining sections have been reproduced, with permission, from the Boston College Career Center.

TRADITIONAL INTERVIEW QUESTIONS
- Tell me about yourself (in two minutes).
- Why do you feel that you will be successful in ...?
- Why did you decide to interview with our organization?
- Why did you choose your major?
- Tell me about your scholastic record.
- What course do you like best? Least? Why?
- Tell me about your extra-curricular activities and interests.
- What have been your most satisfying and most disappointing school or work experiences?
- What did you learn from your part-time or summer job experiences?
- What supervisory or leadership roles have you held?
- What are your strengths and weaknesses?

- Do you have plans for graduate study?
- How do you spend your spare time?
- Why should we hire you?
- Describe briefly your philosophy of education, or nursing, etc.
- Tell me about your practice teaching, or clinical experiences, etc.
- Why did you choose to become a teacher, nurse, etc....?
- How would your last supervisor describe you?
- Where do you see yourself in 5 years? 10 years?
- Do you think your grades are a good indication of your academic achievements?
- How do you work under pressure?
- Why do you want to leave your current job? (If employed full-time.)
- Describe one or two achievements which have given you the most satisfaction.
- In what ways would you contribute to our organization?

BEHAVIORAL INTERVIEW QUESTIONS

Tell me about a time when you . .

- Made a commitment or deadline that was challenged by a personal issue.
- Made a mistake in judgment.
- Worked effectively under pressure.
- Handled a difficult situation with a co-worker.
- Were creative in solving a problem.
- Missed an obvious solution to a problem.
- Were unable to complete a project on time.
- Persuaded team members to do things your way.
- Wrote a report that was well received.
- Anticipated potential problems and developed preventive measures.
- Had to make an important decision with limited facts.
- Were forced to make an unpopular decision.
- Had to adapt to a difficult situation.
- Were tolerant of an opinion that was different from yours.
- Were disappointed in your behavior.
- Had to deal with an irate customer.
- Delegated a project effectively.
- Surmounted a major obstacle.
- Set your sights too high (or too low).
- Prioritized the elements of a complicated project.
- Got bogged down in the details of a project.
- Made a bad decision.
- Turned down a good job.

APPENDIX D
COMPENSATION DATA

This section of the appendix provides detailed compensation data based on Intern Bridge research. The compensation data listed here has been sorted by the student's academic major, the position they held within a host organization, and the various industries in which they interned. The compensation data is unique in that it is "as reported by students," as opposed to most compensation data, which is "as reported by organizations."

COMPENSATION DATA BY MAJOR

Major	N	Hourly
Accounting	99	$15.48
Agriculture	1	$10.50
Anthropology	2	$10.38
Architecture	38	$11.77
Athletic Training	1	$11.00
Biology	38	$10.49
Chemistry	9	$12.83
Communications	40	$10.58
Computer Science	29	$15.03
Creative Writing	1	$10.00
Criminal Justice	4	$10.38
Design	13	$11.19
Earth Sciences	10	$10.23
Economics	48	$14.39
Education	21	$12.32
Engineering	129	$14.29
English Studies	13	$11.06
Ethnic Studies	1	$15.50
Fashion	7	$9.64
Finance	119	$13.80
Fine Art	2	$10.50
Forestry	1	$10.00
Geography	1	$8.00

Major	N	Hourly
Graphic Design	4	$9.00
Health Sciences	16	$10.91
History	16	$10.91
Human Resources	4	$10.38
Hospitality Management	8	$9.16
Humanities	3	$10.50
Human Services	5	$9.00
Information Services	11	$12.23
Law	4	$12.38
Library and Information Science	2	$11.50
Linguistics	2	$14.50
Management	80	$13.28
Marketing	88	$13.28
Mathematics	6	$12.83
Medicine	14	$10.68
Music	1	$9.00
Philosophy	6	$11.25
Physics	6	$8.08
Political Science	31	$10.96
Psychology	20	$11.00
Religion Studies	5	$9.50
Sociology	13	$10.13
Sports Science	2	$8.13
Theatre	3	$8.67
Veterinary Studies	1	$14.25
Other	37	$10.55
Other Business	35	$11.36
Other Science	14	$10.55

COMPENSATION DATA BY INDUSTRY

Industry	N	Hourly
Accounting	68	$16.69
Agriculture/Farming/Agribusiness	7	$13.57
Arts and Entertainment	25	$8.80
Biotechnology	32	$11.15
Communications/Media - Advertising	15	$11.02
Communications/Media - Journalism	4	$7.00
Communications/Media - Marketing/PR	33	$10.15
Communications/Media - Publishing/Print Media	7	$9.43
Communications/Media - TV/Radio Broadcasting	5	$10.85
Consulting - Environmental	3	$12.33
Consulting - Healthcare	6	$15.13
Consulting - Policy	1	$15.00
Consulting - Strategic/Change	12	$13.15
Consulting - Technology	9	$15.61
Consumer Products	16	$14.17
Defense	15	$15.37
Education/Academia	37	$11.88
Energy/Utilities	17	$12.91
Environment	25	$10.42
Finance/Banking - Asset Management	32	$14.15
Finance/Banking - Brokerage	7	$13.57
Finance/Banking - Commercial Banking	12	$12.96
Finance/Banking - Consumer/Retail Banking	10	$12.15
Finance/Banking - Corporate Finance	21	$17.31
Finance/Banking - Services/Planning	37	$11.90
Finance/Banking - Venture Capital	3	$11.33
Government - Federal	21	$10.74
Government - State	15	$10.27
Government - Local	14	$9.71
Healthcare	38	$11.18
Hospitality	19	$9.78
Human Resources	9	$11.56
Insurance	28	$13.94
Legal Services	19	$12.25

Industry	N	Hourly
Manufacturing	42	$14.13
Non-Profit	30	$8.93
Pharmaceutical	16	$12.53
Real Estate	18	$13.29
Retail/Manufacturing	38	$11.93
Social/Human Services	7	$10.21
Technology - Electronics	20	$15.70
Technology - Hardware	8	$17.41
Technology - Information Services	32	$12.93
Technology - Internet/E-commerce	4	$12.56
Technology - Network Administration	7	$12.57
Technology - Software	18	$15.38
Telecommunications	6	$10.88
Transportation	22	$11.28
Other	143	$11.69

COMPENSATION DATA BY POSITION

Position	N	Hourly
Accounting/Auditing	85	$15.47
Actuarial	4	$13.25
Administrative/Support Services	32	$10.28
Analyst	26	$13.73
Brand Management	3	$9.17
Broadcasting	2	$8.75
Business Development	12	$12.65
Buying/Purchasing	6	$12.25
Computer Drafting and Design	24	$11.47
Consulting	15	$14.63
Counseling	6	$10.42
Customer Service	16	$9.56
Cyber Security	2	$18.88
Database Management	7	$12.57
Education	21	$12.24

Total Internship Management

Position	N	Hourly
Engineering	114	$14.34
Event Planning	6	$9.75
Farming/Agriculture	3	$9.17
Finance	91	$13.74
Fundraising/Development	7	$8.64
Hotel/Restaurant/Hospitality	12	$9.02
Human Resources	29	$11.71
Information Management/MIS	7	$11.50
Investigation	1	$16.00
IT/Systems	46	$12.95
Law	19	$12.42
Law Enforcement/Security	4	$11.63
Library Science	3	$11.00
Management	32	$14.62
Marketing	65	$11.27
Medicine	24	$11.30
Operations	36	$12.66
Political Organization/Lobbying	4	$8.00
Product Management	6	$15.83
Programming/Software Development	10	$17.05
Project Management	22	$13.34
Public Relations	22	$9.31
Research	60	$10.93
Sales	44	$12.10
Supply Chain Management/Logistics	3	$11.00
Tax	13	$15.75
Technical Support	8	$15.78
Web Development	7	$10.71
Other	98	$10.90

APPENDIX E
LIST OF RELEVANT ASSOCIATIONS

The following is a list of organizations that you should know about if you are serious about experiential education in your organization.

Cooperative Education and Internship Association
www.CEIA.org

Council for the Advancement of Standards
www.CAS.edu

Eastern Association of Colleges and Employers
www.EACE.org

Midwest Association of Colleges and Employers
www.MWACE.org

Mountain Pacific Association of Colleges and Employers
www.MPACE.org

National Association of Colleges and Employers
www.NACEWEB.org

National Commission for Cooperative Education
www.NCCE.org

National Society for Experiential Education
www.NSEE.org

Southern Association of Colleges and Employers
www.SOACE.org

World Association for Cooperative Education
www.WACEINC.org

Please note that it is highly likely that your state has its own internship association. An internet search should yield the contact information for the folks who manage the group.

Our research and publications can only be as good as your feedback.

If you have any questions or comments, please do not hesitate to contact us by emailing: TheGuide@InternBridge.com.

We guarantee a personal response to each and every email.

Did you know that Intern Bridge provides consulting services, expert speakers, and customized workshops?

Contact us for more information:

www.internbridge.com
1.800.531.6091
Info@InternBridge.com